BUILD YOUR DREAM TEAM

LEADERSHIP BASED ON A PASSION FOR PEOPLE

A PRACTICAL GUIDE FOR PROFESSIONALS
WITHOUT MANAGEMENT TRAINING

Candela Iglesias Chiesa, Ph.D.

ISBN: 978-82-690720-0-6

To Gard

To my family

Contents

Notes on names

The majority of the examples cited in this book are real; when they are made up, I have duly noted it. In order to protect the privacy of the individuals mentioned in the examples of this book, all names have been changed unless explicit permission to use the person's name was granted to me.

Download the Workbook

This book has a companion exercise book that you can download for free from the link below. You don't need to read the workbook to understand this book. However, I would recommend trying the exercises in the companion workbook, particularly in areas where you are dealing with specific challenges. Throughout this book I point out which exercises or "clinics" in the workbook pertain to a specific section.

www.candela-iglesias.com/workbook

Is this book for you?

You've landed a fabulous new job. You've been appointed team leader and are excited to start! But when the first day comes, it's a nightmare.

You went in that morning so happy and enthusiastic, installed yourself in your comfy new office, brought in a plant, your pet's picture and some colourful post-its. Next, of course, you called for a first meeting of your team.

Two people didn't even bother to show up, two others came in late, and spent more time engaged with their smartphones than with you. The only one paying attention was the sweet young intern who couldn't decide if he was feeling sorrier for himself or for you. Worse, every idea you presented to them was met with polite disinterest. By the end of the meeting you could tell there wasn't much team spirit to be found and your colleagues were anything but thrilled by your new role as team leader.

As you go out to lunch at a nearby café to drown your misery, you realize you actually have no clue how to be a team leader. Sure, you're great at what you do, and you've been a great team player. But nothing in your professional training taught you how to do this. "This" being putting together a team. Actually, putting together an **amazing** team.

How do you bring together disparate characters and create

something bigger and better than the sum of the parts? How do you achieve the goals you've promised to the organization and to yourself, goals which can only be accomplished through teamwork? Unless you actually studied for a career in management or business administration, chances are you were never taught anything about team leadership and managing people.

You're not alone. The truth is this is the way many university systems work: they churn out highly-specialized individuals who are extremely competent in their area of knowledge. But they leave out key transferable skills that most of us will need at some point during our careers.

Thus, we have doctors, designers, lawyers, scientists, marketers, nurses, teachers, sociologists, artists, economists, and others, who, because they're great at what they do, are at some point in their careers assigned to a leadership position and put in charge of a team. If we get lucky, our company or organization will give us a one-to-three-day course in team leadership and management. Most of the time, though, we go in with nothing but our own skill-set and passion.

Sound familiar? This book is for you if:

a.   You have just started as a team leader (at work, in a sport or a hobby, or when volunteering) but have never learned about leadership and management in your career.

b.   You have been a leader for a while but are currently facing a crisis period and feel you don't have the tools to resolve it or if you want to learn new ways to strengthen your team, get better results, and build a better work environment.

If you're at one of these points in your life, things might be looking tough. I've been there. I was a researcher thrown into a leadership position. This book draws on lessons I learned while bringing together professionals to create a team. I'm sharing everything I read, researched and tested on that journey.

Years ago, when I returned to my home country, after a spell spent abroad, my boss tasked me with putting together a team. I was incredibly excited about the idea, until I realized the constrictions under which I had to set up this team.

First, I had no power over who would become a team member and who wouldn't (i.e., hiring decisions were not up to me). Second, I had no power over who could stay on the team or who had to leave (i.e., firing decisions were also not up to me). Third, the people who were going to become members of this team had, until now, been happily working quite independently with very little oversight or teamwork.

As if these constraints weren't enough, I was also dealing with some confidence issues. While I had led small groups of students and assistants in the past, I had never coordinated a large team of skilled professionals. I was sure I was going be called out as a fraud, fail splendidly, and showcase in big red letters how unsuited I was to leading a team of smart, hands-on, independent professionals.

But I'm not one to say no to a new challenge, I was really passionate about the work we were doing and convinced that bringing people together would allow us to serve our beneficiaries so much better. So, I went for it.

By the time I left, all my team members had completed or were in a graduate degree (or even two) while working full-time. They had achieved team and individual goals they had never expected were possible some years ago. Now, they are becoming leaders in their own right. They still use (and perfect) the tools I shared with them and many keep in touch regularly. To me that is the best reward of all.

Because I've trained as a researcher, every time I've been confronted with a new problem, my first reaction has been to hide behind a book. It provides good cover while allowing me to read up and research on how to solve this new situation. However, during this journey, I have struggled with the lack of a handy how-to guide for building a dream team. I have read many great books on leadership and organizational behaviour, but I found few good practical books on team-building. And so this book was born.

This book is meant to show you all the skills you already possess for putting together a dream team, and how to build on them. It is intended to be a step-by-step guide to keep you company through this new, exciting journey. (You can also hide behind it if need be!) You can read the book from start to finish or go directly to the sections that speak to the specific challenge you are facing right now.

After reading this book and testing the practical ideas in it, within weeks you'll see positive changes in how your team relates to you and to each other. You'll feel empowered. You'll have a clear vision of who you want to be as a leader and what you want your dream team to look like, and most importantly, the tools and the plan that will make that vision a reality.

With time, the current composition of your team will become a thrilling challenge instead of a dreary weight holding you back from achieving your team's goals, the inevitable conflicts a stimulating opportunity to try out your conflict-solving toolkit.

My goal with this book is that you will find simple, easily-implementable solutions to the problems that now seem insurmountable. That tomorrow, after reading the chapter on conflict, you will not again go to work with a knot in your stomach knowing Peter is angry at Jane and, since they're not talking to each other, the project is in jeopardy. That instead of dreading your team meetings, you'll start looking forward to interacting with your team. That when the next quarter comes, you'll have a clear plan of how to create an amazing opportunity out of those dull personnel reviews. That in a few weeks from now, the grey cloud of dread, boredom, and stress hanging over you every Monday morning when you have to hit the office will disappear and the sky will look bright blue as you go re-join that dream team of yours for another week of astounding successes.

The journey starts here. It's a fun one.

WHAT IS A LEADER?

When I was barely twenty-two years old, I had the opportunity to spend a day at a "leadership camp" in the middle of the forest. We were thrown together with complete strangers in ten-person teams and presented with a series of challenges to accomplish in a certain time-span. The challenges included walking on cables suspended between trees, balancing a huge see-saw, jumping from a cliff to be carried away on a zip line, and the classic soldier's task of getting the whole team up and over a tall wall.

At the end of the day, they made us choose a leader from among our team members. Our team chose two. The voting was very clear; people knew exactly who had helped the most with getting the whole team through all the obstacles. These people were not necessarily the bravest, the loudest, or the bossiest.

They were the ones who organized us all. They appointed people to direct each task, so that everyone wasn't talking at the same time. They motivated people. They asked others to respect the directives of the people in charge of that task. They went back to the ones falling behind and helped them catch up to the rest of the team.

So it seems, when we're part of a team, we know, instinctively, who our leaders are. Who are these people? What do they have or do that makes us give them this label?

Sometimes they're our managers; sometimes they are not.

Sometimes they have an official title; sometimes they don't. In my view, what they share is a clear, inspiring vision and a passion for their team.

Much has been written about the distinction between leadership and management. Part of this distinction is attributed to the clarity of the vision they have. To illustrate this, let me share with you a forest metaphor I first read in Stephen Covey's long-time bestseller *The Seven Habits of Highly Effective People*.[1]

Imagine a team is cutting a path through a dense forest. They're trying to get to the clearing on the other side, where a prized pot of gold stands--the goal. This team is made up of the problem-solvers, the "hands-on" people. The manager is the person behind them, ensuring they have tools to hack away at the undergrowth, organizing the clearing schedules, and worrying that they've already spent more time than was planned. She sees very clearly that the next obstacle is going to be a big boulder smack in the middle of the path the team has been clearing and how tired two of the team members are getting. She can't see the next obstacle and has no clear view of the pot of gold in the clearing. Her thoughts are focused on the day-to-day.

The leader is the person who is standing at the top of the tallest tree with a full view of the landscape. She sees the clearing with the pot of gold. She can tell the team how amazing it looks. She sees all the obstacles and challenges in the way. She sees the team, working as a whole. She also realizes they are trying to hack through the forest on the widest side and they need to change paths.

This metaphor highlights the importance of a vision, of the overall picture against the day-to-day, when distinguishing between a leader and a manager. This vision allows the leader not only to strategize better in the long term but also to inspire the team by sharing that vision. Of course, it is possible to be a great leader and manager at the same time. They are by no means mutually exclusive.

In my own view, a leader not only has a clear overview of the landscape and the ultimate goals, but she also believes that her team can overcome the obstacles--clear a path through the forest--by themselves with adequate support and guidance and is thus interested in helping them grow to achieve that goal. She is interested not only in attaining the objectives of the organization but also in helping each individual grow and fulfil their potential. A manager will be more concerned with meeting deadlines, maintaining budgets, and ensuring efficiency in day-to-day tasks and less concerned with the people in her team.

In other words, to me the distinction lies not only in where your vision lies but also where your passion lies. I believe great leaders are passionate about people. Yes, they care deeply about the goals, but it's because they care so passionately about people that their teams can see the beauty of the shared goal and become deeply committed to achieving it.

And don't think that because your title is "project manager" or "programme coordinator" you can't be this kind of passionate leader. You might not have any leadership or management title whatsoever and still be doing the heavy lifting for your organization in terms of leading a team. Don't wait for permission. Don't wait for a title. If you have that passion and that vision, dive right in and start acting as a leader. The rest will come.

Margie Warrell, speaker and author of "Stop Playing Safe," said it best in one of her Forbes columns: "You don't need a title to be a leader, and you don't need to wait for permission. You just need the courage to take action and the patience to wait for others to realize you're a force to be reckoned with!"[2]

* * *

This book is divided into four parts, set in a logical sequence. The first part, "As Things Stand," is about your starting point. Identifying the leadership skills you already possess and the myths about leadership that you believe in, which may be holding you back. Then we move on to mapping out your team and your organization, clarifying your areas of influence, and how you can expand them.

Because in order to successfully lead a team we first need to be able to lead ourselves efficiently, in the second part "Leading You," we'll move to growing your leadership skill set, both in terms of "people" skills and of planning and time-management strategies.

In the third part, "Leading your Team," I'll walk you through the process that individuals who are asked to work together with others go through in order to become a team. We'll discuss how you can influence this process in a positive way to facilitate the creation of a cohesive, effective team.

Now that you've set up a strong team, what can you do in the day-to-day to keep this great team on track? Communication is what makes or breaks a team. We'll discuss common challenges, along with formal and informal strategies you can set up from day one to enhance good communication.

Finally, in the fourth section, we'll tackle conflict. Because no matter how good your team is, no matter how strong your communication strategies are, conflict *will* arise. Here we'll talk about how to tackle it proactively, to ensure that never does a day arrive when you are dreading going to work because the tensions and resentments have grown unbearable. You'll learn effective strategies to deal with intrapersonal and interpersonal conflict.

This book can be read sequentially, which is what I would recommend, but you can also skip to the particular section that relates to the area where you are having issues. For example, it can be hard to focus on defining the values of your team when the underlying conflict is boiling to the surface every day. In that case, go to the end of the book first and try out the conflict-solving techniques. Once conflict levels have subsided, you'll be more able to focus on strengthening your leadership skills or team-building strategies, and you can go back to read the foundational sections.

One last word: none of this is rocket science. Which means all of us can do it. We can all become better leaders and build stronger teams. It is a matter of being humble enough to identify our gaps and areas of opportunity but also aware enough to recognize our existing strengths. Leaders don't discount their own abilities nor those of others. They firmly believe they can grow themselves and their teams.

PART I

AS THINGS STAND

Chapter 1
You as a leader

When I was charged with putting together a team of specialists, I kept thinking over and over for the first few weeks: "They will never accept my leadership. They are experts in their own field, and I'm not an expert in those fields! What gives me the right to lead them?"

Because of this belief, I tried to make it all about experience: I was older. I had more experience. I had worked in different countries and settings. I had a broader and deeper understanding of our organization. Of course, all of these were true and, to a certain degree, they did give me an edge, allowing me to contribute something important to the team.

But these experience-based contributions were not, in the end, the reason my boss had chosen me for the job. They were just my poor attempts at rationalizing around a deeply-held conviction that I had no "right" to lead a team of specialists in a field where I was not specialised. Basically, I believed the myth: "I need to be the expert to be the leader."

I have heard many other myths about what it takes to be a leader. Some believe they can't be a leader because they aren't in a certain position in their organization or because they lack experience or because they are too young, too introverted, and so on. Yet, over the years I have come to the conclusion that there is not a single "right" recipe for leadership.

In this chapter, we'll look at the different types of effective leadership, discussing the different sources of leadership power and myths about what it takes to be a leader. We'll discuss why the mentality we have around growth can be more important than traits or skills, and we'll finish with an exercise helping you to identify various skills commonly associated with leadership.

THERE ARE DIFFERENT TYPES OF EFFECTIVE LEADERSHIP

In management and organizational behaviour courses, they teach students that leadership power can come from various sources, and different personality types can give rise to great leaders. For those of us coming from non-managerial professional backgrounds, this knowledge can help dispel common myths surrounding leadership and provide a wider view on who can become a leader.

Sources of leadership power

John French and Bertrand Raven, back in 1959, researched the sources of power that leaders use to influence others.[3] They identified five sources of power. Three categorized as "organizational power": legitimate (or position power), coercive power, and reward power. Two categorized as "personal power": expert power and referent power. Today organizational management theorists have added two more, connection power and informational power.

Legitimate (or position) power stems from your work title. For example, if you're officially labelled as a manager, a team leader, or a department director in your organization's hierarchy.

Coercive power comes from your authority to hire and fire individuals, discount working days or hours, or other punitive measurements.

Reward power, on the other hand, stems from your authority to give raises, promotions or awards. While these may be good motivators, a good leader who has no access to these will still find ways to motivate her team.

Connection power has to do with who you know and the influence you obtain in other people's eyes by knowing this person or having this connection. It is a power type commonly used in politics. Connections and networks are something that any of us can acquire with enough time investment.

Expert power is conferred on you by your knowledge and experience. Or, more precisely, by the knowledge and experience other people *perceive* you to have. It may stem from an academic title of from people recognizing you and recommending you as an expert.

Informational power is when you have information that other people need or want. It tends to be a short-term power. Although, some individuals will hoard and withhold information from others in order to accumulate this power. On the other hand, some people appear to be natural recipients of information, usually because they are social or are good listeners.

Referent power or **personal power** is the ability to make people naturally look to you for advice, guidance, and leadership. It is considered by many researchers as the most valuable source of power. It has to do with an ability to personally influence others because they have admiration, respect, friendship, and similar positive feelings towards you. We tend to think of people with personal power as outgoing and charismatic, but many other personality types can also show this referent power. Think of the shy friend you always go to for sound advice, for instance. This power can be held by anyone willing to put in the work and shoulder the responsibilities of leadership, and the most beautiful thing is that it cannot be taken away by a third party.

So, if like me, you're thinking that you don't have enough experience to be a leader, notice that, of all these different types of power, only one refers to the amount of experience you have--expert power. If you lack specific experience and have been appointed a leader, chances are someone saw one or more of these other sources of leadership power in you.

These varied sources of power also highlight something we mentioned in the introduction--you don't need a title to be a leader. Only one of the seven types of leadership power actually requires you to have a position of authority: position power (and to a lesser extent coercive and reward power). Your leadership power can stem from many other sources. We all know that charismatic person in our teams who is not the official team leader but exerts a great deal of influence on everybody.

Leadership and personal traits

Other concerns surrounding leadership focus on whether we have the right "personality," to be a leader, whether we are too young for it, or--unbelievable but still true in the 21st century--whether our sex impacts our ability to be a leader. Below I'll briefly discuss these myths.

Myth. Leaders are extroverts. When it comes to personality, shy or introverted people, in particular, tend to worry about whether they will do well in a leadership position. They may worry that they are not magnetic or charismatic enough, or that they don't like to be seen.

Yet, the world abounds with examples of introverts who are great leaders. Susan Cain, in her book *Quiet: The Power of Introverts in A World That Can't Stop Talking*, argues that Warren Buffet, the business magnate, and Rosa Parks, the civil rights activist, fit the introvert category, and despite that, they are both are seen as leaders in their areas.[4]

We might not hear as much about introvert leaders, precisely because of their personality type, but their teams love them to death, nevertheless. A case in point is my former colleague, who I'll call Sam. Over the ten years I've known him, I've seen him in his introvert manner gain a reputation for himself as a solid researcher and team leader without ever showcasing himself.

He has a great number of students and staff working in his projects, but you will still see him doing tedious, repetitive tasks because he finds it unfair to ask others on his team to do things he is not willing to do. I've never seen him raise his voice, but he is earnest in his quiet anger when defending his team members if he thinks an unfairness has been committed. Everybody loves him , partly because he's an introvert, because despite his brilliance he is so humble and self-effacing. He's had no need to showcase himself because the respect and admiration he's earned from his team and peers lead other people do all the showcasing for him.

Myth. I'm too nice to be a leader. Other people worry that they might not be "tough" enough to be leaders. I did. I was uncomfortable with the idea of imposing my own viewpoint on my team, but I was scared that by being too inclusive I would "lose control" of my team and things wouldn't get done.

The truth is, in many environments nowadays, the old, hierarchical, bureaucratic structures associated with the 20th century have given way to much flatter organizational structures. This has profoundly changed the way teams are managed.

Many 21st-century workplaces are about consensus and participation. Leaders may be responsible for setting the **what**-- the goals, and the deadlines. But participatory approaches are used for the **how's**--how will we get there, how can each of us contribute. Teams brainstorm ideas on the best ways to achieve the goals and people volunteer to take up the different tasks.

Daniel Pink, in his book *Drive*, argues that in many modern workplaces, productivity rises and employees and organizations thrive when intrinsic motivation, not a "carrot and stick" punishment and reward system, is the driving force.[5] This means that we should worry less about being "tough" and more about understanding how to motivate and inspire our teams.

Myth. I'm too young to be a leader. Another prevailing myth surrounding leadership is the feeling that age, especially youth, makes a difference. Let's look at some counter-examples. Malala Yousafzai was seventeen when she won the Nobel Peace Prize and barely fifteen when she was shot by Taliban gunmen due to the leadership and courage she had shown in matters of girl's education.[6] Mark Zuckerberg was nineteen-years-old when he launched Facebook and not even thirty when Facebook went public, raising sixteen billion dollars[7].

In our hyper-connected world, examples of young leaders abound. I wrote this book with the support of a superb writing and publishing program created by a twenty-something.[8] Probably over 90% of his students are older than he is.

Some of these young leaders may seem like unreachable Hollywood type stories; yet, many are just common teenagers or young adults who decided to step up. Deciding to lead is a choice we can make at any age.

Young leaders will tend to have more personal or connection power than other types of power, as they may not have much experience, knowledge, or skills yet, and they may be students, interns or hold junior positions, which do not come with much position, coercive, or reward power.

Myth. Men are natural leaders, women are not. It is sad that in this day and age I even need to address this myth. Yet, it's still a highly pervasive belief. Fortunately, more and more female role models of great leadership are appearing who we can look up to for inspiration. Think Angela Merkel, the German chancellor; Margaret Chan, the head of the World Health Organization; Hillary Rodham Clinton, the U.S. senator, secretary of state and presidential candidate; Christine Lagarde, the head of the International Monetary Fund (IMF). NASA's latest class of astronauts is 50% female. And, if you think certain areas such as tech or automobile industry are not for women, there's Marissa Meyer, the CEO of Yahoo; Sheryl Sandberg, the COO of Facebook; Mary Barra, CEO of General Motors; and Susan Wojcicki, CEO of YouTube, among many others.

Out of the spotlight of the highest leadership positions, a number of studies suggest that women rate as effective as men as leaders, even though one gender may prevail over the other in particular industry categories and the genders show differences in leadership traits.[9] With the rise of women to positions of power, negative myths and beliefs about women's leadership are quickly being dispelled.

Negative beliefs surrounding women's leadership abilities come not only from society-at-large but also from conscious and unconscious beliefs held by women themselves. If you're a woman struggling with these issues, you will find recommendations for further reading in the Notes and Resources section of this book.[10]

If you're interested in looking more closely into the various myths surrounding leadership and any perceived limitations you may have on your ability to become a leader, Clinic 1 the Workbook has an exercise based on these myths to help you identify which ones are holding you back.

LEADERSHIP CAN BE LEARNT

Along with all the myths discussed above, another common belief is that leaders are born, not made. Meaning either you're cut out for a leadership job or you're not, and there's nothing you can do about it. However, there is strong data to suggest otherwise. You can actually do plenty about it.

Carol Dweck, a renowned Stanford University psychologist explains in her book, *Mindset,* the difference between a fixed and growth mentality.[11] Based on many years of research, she shows that individuals with a "fixed mindset" believe that intelligence or talent are fixed traits that cannot be changed, so the only thing to do is measure them. This is also the idea behind the "leaders are born, not made" belief.

Individuals with a "growth mindset," on the other hand, believe they can improve their abilities, developing their minds through hard work and perseverance. While intelligence or talent are indeed important, these traits do not define us. For example, a person with a fixed mindset would say "I'm not a runner," and thus not even start training to become a runner, while someone with a growth mindset would say, "I've never run before, but I'm sure I can run that race if I train hard."

Importantly, Dweck has shown that the belief you hold--whether a fixed or growth mindset--(and of course, most of us are some mixture of the two) deeply affects your performance in life and whether you work towards your goals and dreams and becoming the person you want to be. Students and workers in different experimental settings who believe that skills and traits can be learned have been able to acquire new skills, while this has proven more difficult for those with a fixed mindset.

The good news about a growth mindset is that experiments have shown it can be taught. When individuals are taught about the growth mindset concept, they exhibit higher productivity and success in areas such as business, education, and sports.

This body of research suggests that leaders are not necessarily born, and can definitely be made. While some individuals may have some natural talents or personality traits that facilitate their way to leadership or have grown up in an environment that promotes leadership, we can all learn leadership skills and keep becoming better leaders. We can start from where we are and grow ourselves while growing our teams.

YOU ARE NOT STARTING FROM ZERO

A growth mindset allows us to develop skills for leadership. In our quest to become stronger leaders, however, we are rarely, if ever, starting from zero.

You already possess and have shown leadership characteristics in one area or other of your life. Identifying these instances provides a starting platform, clarifying areas of strengths and highlighting areas of opportunity where you can focus your learning on leadership.

Some years ago, I used to run workshops where we trained people to become lay counsellors. One of the first things we would do was a skill identification exercise. We would first launch a discussion of the general traits and skills that participants believed a counsellor required. Things like "good listening skills," "empathy," and "strength" usually came up.

Then we'd ask the participants to come up with an instance where they had shown each of those traits or skills. When people got stuck, we clarified that examples could be drawn not only from professional but also from personal life. That normally made a difference. Many people had shown a number of these traits before in their personal lives, but because they had been thinking only inside the professional sphere, they were unable to acknowledge that they had these skills.

Here we'll do a similar exercise. Below you will see a list of skills commonly associated with leadership,[12] followed by examples of that skill. Feel free to add additional skills that you consider important for leadership.

The goal of the exercise is for *every one* of these skills to think of one example, at least one, where you've shown that skill or trait. Think about your work. Think about your home, with your family, your friends, or a stranger. Think back to when you were a kid, a teenager, a college student. Any instance counts.

If you're thinking that you have all the patience in the world with your kids, but you'll never be that patient with team workers or colleagues, well, maybe you are right. Then again, we are also hoping your team members and colleagues won't act like tantrum-throwing toddlers. In any case, you've shown this particular trait at some point. You have a base on which to build that skill and make it work in your professional sphere. Skills are transferable.

In the Workbook associated with this book, you'll find an exercise sheet with space to write down your examples for each trait in Clinic 2.

LEADERSHIP SKILLS
Assertiveness
- Making your point emphatically without aggressiveness.
Awareness
- Being able to adapt your approach or message to different people and situations.
- Being sensible to other people's feelings.
Communication
- Listening actively without interrupting.
- Asking questions that inspire insights in the other person.
- Showing empathy to a person in distress.
- Clearly transmitting a complex idea to another person.

Confidence

- Believing setbacks are normal on the path towards your goal.
- Trusting you or your team have or can learn the abilities to complete a certain goal.

Conflict-solving

- Diffusing a difficult or tense situation.
- Responding calmly and constructively when someone is verbally aggressive to you.
- Taking criticism as feedback and not as a personal attack.

Cooperation

- Working well with others.
- Willingness to let others participate in tasks and share the credit.
- Providing information and support to others so that a task is achieved.

Decision-making

- Making a decision with very little information.
- Gathering information, consulting different viewpoints before making a decision.
- Coming up with more than two options for every decision.

Delegating

- Trusting someone to do a good job without your close supervision.
- Capitalizing on other people's strengths.

Flexibility

- Expecting to change course in the middle of a process as new information comes in.
- Keeping calm and maintaining a sense of humour when several things go wrong at the same time.

Learning

- Learning how to do better after making a mistake.

- Challenging yourself by learning something new.

Mentoring/Coaching

- Providing advice that was considered useful by the other person.
- Teaching someone a new way to do something.
- Supporting people in their growth

Motivating and inspiring

- Convincing someone they can do something they didn't think was possible for them.
- Inspiring people to do a difficult or boring task with good humour.

Proactivity/Initiative

- Not waiting for others to tell you what to do.
- Proposing and taking action.

Problem-solving

- Knowing where to find information and support to find a solution.
- Bringing people's strengths together in order to solve a problem
- Providing a different perspective to a problem, which facilitates finding a solution.

Professionalism

- Being there on time, keeping a deadline.
- Keeping calm when things trigger you.
- Keeping a cool head when everybody else is upset.
- Delivering on your promises.

Responsibility

- Accepting responsibility for a mistake you made.
- Sharing credit where it is due.
- Stepping up to take charge when needed.

Strategic thinking

- Seeing further ahead than everyone else.
- Understanding how current actions will or will not move

you towards your long term goal.

- Anticipating a problem and planning for it.
- Questioning and critically thinking around a commonly-held idea or belief.
- Finding more than one possible explanation or solution.

How did you do? Were you able to identify an example for each? If you didn't, keep in mind that many of us have a hard time remembering our strong points. You may want to ask a trusted colleague, friend, or family member.

Hopefully, this exercise has allowed you to identify existing strengths, which you can transfer to your job and develop further for your new leadership position, while also highlighting potential areas of opportunity on which you can focus your growth.

This is your starting point. You're not starting from zero. In several avenues of your life, you've shown skills or traits that are linked to leadership. You can repurpose these for your new team leadership position.

* * *

In this chapter, we've discussed the notion that successful leaders come in many different types. We can use our own voice. We are not starting from zero, and we already possess skills that provide a good starting point for our new leadership positions. And, if we cultivate a growth mindset, any traits or skills we think we need to improve our leadership, we can learn.

In the next chapter, we will move the spotlight from you to your surrounding environment. We will focus on analysing the organization you work for or you lead, and the people in it, to clarify your zones of influence.

Chapter 2
Your environment

CLAUDIA is an architect and has her own business. In theory, she can shape her company, as she wants and focus on the projects she prefers. Because it's a small company, the structure is very flat. She has hiring and firing power over her staff. Claudia represents one end of the spectrum, small business owners who can pretty much shape the environment of their company as they wish, as long as they have or can create the resources to do it.

In the middle of the spectrum, Darragh works for a medium-sized NGO (non-governmental organization, not-for-profit or charity) focused on education. He is in charge of programmes helping teenagers. He has a lot of leeway to create projects and interventions as he sees fit, as long as they show good results, which contribute toward the main goal and are in line with the budget. Within the scope of his budget, he can move budget categories around. He has a team but has no hiring or firing power over them. At most, he can suggest that someone is not working adequately or show that he needs an extra person and try to convince the boss to hire a new team member. His team is composed not only of highly-skilled and motivated people who are used to working autonomously but also of volunteers who require a lot of supervision.

At the other end of the spectrum, Mai is a medical doctor working for a big pharmaceutical company. The structure is very hierarchical. All processes are highly bureaucratic with checks and balances at every step. Her team expects to be told what to do in precise detail. In theory, she can influence hiring and firing decisions as far as her team is concerned; although, she has many constraints due to the associated costs. Any new idea, project, or change in the budget requires a lengthy process to be evaluated and possibly accepted. The way she interacts with other departments is also highly-structured and coded.

Claudia, Darragh, and Mai are all experts in their fields who have little or no formal managerial or leadership training and are in leadership positions in very different organizations. They're examples of the wide spectrum of organizational environments in which you might be expected to lead a team.

If we compare your leadership quest to climbing a mountain, your skills, which we've already discussed, are all the useful tools you will be carrying when attempting the climb, and the organizational environment you are in would be the mountain you are climbing: the weather, the paths, and the boulders you will have to endure and the team you are bringing along for the climb.

Much in the same way as you would pour over maps and weather forecasts before climbing a mountain, it is useful to spend a little while analysing your organization's environment when you are starting as a team leader.

YOUR ORGANIZATION

In terms of your organization, you may want to identify the things you can change, the things you can influence, and the things over which you have no control. I like to call these three zones: your "decision-making zone," your "zone of influence," and the "far beyond." You can visualize them as three concentric spheres, with your decision-making zone being the inner one.

In Clinic 3 in the Workbook, you will have an opportunity to identify items in your three zones and brainstorm ways you can expand your reach from the innermost sphere to the two circles beyond.

Sphere 1: Your decision-making zone

Your decision-making zone is where you are in charge. Spend some time identifying exactly which issues are under your control and where you can make any final decisions.

First, clarify which hiring and firing decisions are up to you and how much organizational leeway you have. For example, Claudia, the architect and business owner, has complete hiring and firing power over her team. While Mai, working for a big pharma, needs to work together with HR and her bosses on any hiring or firing decision.

What about your organization? Are there pre-set HR review processes in your company or can you set up your own? Can you fire people who are not working as needed? Can you, on the other hand, keep someone who's way of work you like despite your boss calling for his or her dismissal? Can you hire new people if it is inside your budget? If someone is hired, will it be you who does the hiring process and interviews, you who has the final call?

Then, look into the amount of influence you have over your team, e.g., can you, with their consent, rearrange the way they work, shift them from one project to another, switch their office arrangements, move around their schedules? Darragh, working with the educational NGO, has quite some leeway in shifting tasks from one volunteer to another, for instance.

Now look into the amount of power you have over your projects. Can you design new projects or interventions as long as they are in line with the company or department goals? Do you have to stick to a pre-agreed plan? Can you be creative inside that plan? Can you choose which clients to work with?

For example, Darragh is known for coming up with new projects when he identifies new needs in his beneficiaries. Claudia can get creative inside the wishes of her client's dream home project.

Finally, consider your decision-making power over your budget. Can you ask for a particular budget yearly? Do you earn your own budget? Are you completely restricted by the allocated budget or can you move things around if plans change?

Write down any and all decisions in all categories that are up to you. Make a note about any that you're not sure if you can make a final call on, and ask.

Sphere 2: Your influence zone

Your influence zone is where you *don't* rule but where you can have a good amount of influence in the outcome. Normally this sphere encompasses your boss, especially if you have a good relationship with her and she trusts you, your team, many of your colleagues; and your clients or beneficiaries (if you work with them directly and can thus influence them.) Mai, for instance, has a wide influence zone due to the high trust her boss and colleagues have in her.

Sometimes your influence zone includes people in other departments, your boss's boss, the board of directors. What about your level of influence in general company policy? Or with other departments in your organization? Darragh, for instance, working in a medium-sized NGO, knows some people on the board of directors well, providing him with a larger zone of influence.

Your influence zone can include your team composition if you cannot make final decisions but can still influence hiring and firing choices. It may encompass the technical level of your team members if you can help them get more training, motivate them to continue their studies, pay for a workshop, and so on.

When you flesh out your zone of influence, think about all the types of power that we've discussed and how you can use them to expand your sphere. If you create good relationships with people, you'll be expanding your level of influence through people or referent power. If people come to you to freely share information or to ask for advice, you'll be expanding your level of influence through connection or information power. If you are great at listening to clients, your information power will also increase.

Spend some time brainstorming ideas for expanding your decision-making zone into certain items in zone two. Would regular meetings with your boss help? What about sending reports to the board? Could you invite colleagues from other departments to your meetings when appropriate? Could you spend some time getting to know colleagues in HR, admin, finance and IT to understand their functions and processes better and create good working relationships?

Sphere 3: The far beyond

This last sphere is beyond your influence zone, at least for now. It may contain the CEO of the company, the board of directors, possibly a list of clients who you don't have any direct communication with or way of influencing. It can include processes and systems in the company, other departments, office space, rewards, promotions, and sometimes hiring and firing decisions.

Notice that while you may not have any influence on *choosing* the people that are on your team, you can still influence and motivate the people on your team. And while possibly you cannot choose your office space or that of your team, you probably have some amount of leeway on how to furnish and decorate it, even in small ways, or how to rearrange it. Be sure to clearly specify what is *completely* out of your control *right now*. Keep in mind that you can find ways to expand your influence zone and push into this far beyond with time and effort.

What can you do in the medium term to push your influence zone out to encompass items that are now in the far beyond? Could you propose a new organizational system? What about taking on some new responsibilities? Or apply for grants or sources of financing to expand your budget? Write down all your ideas. You can use the space provided in the Workbook if you want.

YOUR TEAM COMPOSITION

Now that you've mapped out the organization, it is time to focus a bit more on those individuals you're going to be working with most closely--your team.

Either you are starting from scratch and you need to put together a team, or you already have a team, or a group of people that are *supposed* to be a team. In either case, it's useful to think about the skills you require on your team depending on the project, your team's goals, and the time you have to achieve those goals. Based on these skills you can identify the type of people you wish to include in your team or the areas in which people will require training or support.

If you are putting together a team

If you're putting together a team from scratch, you need to decide the different skills you'll need. If you work in a big organization, human resources may already have done some of the work for you, and position descriptions may already be available.

In any case, sit down for a while and think through the different skills you'll need from each team member. This way you'll have a clear understanding of what you are looking for when you start interviewing. In Clinic 4 in the Workbook, you'll find a spreadsheet to help you analyse the skills and experience you may require in your team.

Personality is also something you may want to consider when hiring. However, as we will see in detail in later chapters, researchers have found that individual personalities are not as critical to the team culture as the team's own personality as a whole. And your team's emerging personality is something you can influence.

Still, if you now have the opportunity to interview and choose people for your team, make the best of it by ensuring they fulfil particular characteristics you cherish. For example, while I don't care if a person is shy or outgoing, funny or serious, I do care very much that:

a.   They are proactive.
b.   They have a growth mindset.
c.   They are willing and enthusiastic about working in a

team.

d.   They are able to give and receive constructive criticism.

e.   They have a sense of humour.

The things you care about might be very different but spend some time deciding what they are first.

When you interview a prospective candidate for your team, you're trying to answer two questions: first, is this person capable of doing the job he or she will be required to do, and with which level of ability? And second, is this person a good fit for my team and for me?

If you already have a team

Let's say you're a nurse and you have just been promoted to head nurse in a clinic or hospital. You won't be putting together a team from scratch; instead, you will be leading the nurses already working there. In cases like this, where you already have a team, start by getting hold of their resumes and previous evaluations. With this at hand and from your own observations, list the skills and experience each person has and how these would be useful to fulfil the team's goals.

Once you've mapped this out, identify important gaps in skills in your team, and then move on to brainstorm ways to palliate these gaps or decide they'll require a new hire. For example, the clinic has decided that it will be starting an outreach, door-to-door vaccination campaign in the community, and your team is in charge of this. None of the nurses in your team has the exact profile for this, but is there anyone who is passionate about vaccination campaigns or community outreach? Would he be interested in taking up this extra role? Can you outsource this part to a volunteer? Is there someone on the team who may be interested in getting training to fulfil this part? Who would be more suitable?

If instead of choosing your team, the team was chosen for

you and perhaps you feel like you "got stuck" with a team that you aren't sure is up to the required standard, the exercise above becomes key. It can help you let go of your assumptions and objectively identify the skills and experience available, as well as clarify areas of opportunity and requirements for new hires. It'll help you gain respect for your team members, and possibly realize that you don't know as much about them as you think, which is a very good starting point for an honest conversation about their skills and interests.

In Clinic 4 in the Workbook, you will find a table to help you analyse your current team composition.

* * *

Hopefully, after reading this chapter, you have a clearer picture of the environment you'll be working in, your organization and your team members. Sometimes just taking the time to sit down and reflect on this starting point will alleviate some of the anxiety surrounding your new position. Pausing to reflect will also provide clarity about what's under your control going forward, as well as fresh ideas on expanding your areas of influence and addressing the gaps in your team composition.

This brings us to the end of Part I. You have gained clarity on your own starting point by looking into the myths you may have believed about leadership and identifying your strengths and skills. You have mapped the environment you will be working in as well as your team composition.

In Part II we will focus on growing your leadership abilities. We will start by talking about some of the challenges you may encounter when transitioning from a team member to a team leader and discuss ways to make this transition easier. Then we will dive into two sets of leadership skills: the leadership mindset (or soft skills), which has to do with how you relate to people and leadership strategies (or hard skills), such as organizational and time-management skills important to increase your effectiveness and that of your team.

PART II

Leading you

Chapter 3

Positioning Yourself as a Leader

GLENN was a secondary school teacher in a big private school. He had a good relationship with his colleagues and was friends with many of them, seeing them outside of the school as well. One day the principal retired and the board asked Glenn to take over as principal. Glenn was happy for the opportunity and intrigued by the challenge. He knew he had the organizational skills to do the job. He was good at dealing with both parents and teenagers. He knew a couple of the board members and thought he wouldn't have a problem dealing with the rest of them. In short, he believed he was ready to take on this new role.

What he'd never expected was the backlash he got from his colleagues and former team members when he was promoted. Some were supportive. Others didn't bother to hide that they considered themselves better candidates than him for the position. One sweet, soft-spoken English teacher stopped talking to him altogether. The gym teacher, a good friend of Glenn's, took him out for beers to celebrate and then spent the evening telling him about the changes he needed to make in the school. Glenn suddenly realized he needed a strategy to position himself as a new leader and facilitate his transition.

In many instances, for professionals without formal

managerial training, the path to a leadership position may come in a similar manner. While doing your job as a team member someone identified you as a potential leader and you were promoted to lead your former colleagues.

Your opportunity to lead a team may have come in other ways, too. Maybe a new company hired you, or you come from another department in the same company. In these cases, you don't know any of the people you're going to lead. You could be supplanting a well-liked team leader, or a detested one. The team you're now in charge of may have existed previously, in which case you're the newcomer. Or it may have just been formed, in which case most or all of the individuals won't know each other. In any case, you'll need a strategy to ensure a good transition.

DEFINING WHO YOU WANT TO BE AS A LEADER

The important thing at this stage is to decide beforehand what type of leader *you* want to be. Do you care more about effectiveness or creativity? The overall picture or attention to detail? Do you want to be liked too or are you happy enough with reaching the organization's goals? Take some time to reflect on this. In Clinic 5 in the Workbook you will find an exercise that may help you in this reflection.

The type of leader you will be not only has to do with your personality and skills but also with the organization (the environment) you are working in. Obviously, it would be difficult to maintain strict military-style discipline in an extremely creative and flat organizational structure. On the other hand, if you have a team who is used to being told exactly what to do, they may find themselves at a loss when you ask them to be creative and autonomous.

The style of connection you can have with your team members depends as much on them as it does on you. However, knowing from the start what type of connection *you* want will help you steer your relationship with them towards the type of connection you are aiming for.

You may also wish to think about how would you like your team to be seen from the outside. Do you care more about being perceived as an effective team? A team who always meets deadlines? A creative team? The problem-solvers? A hard-working team? Do you want to put together the fun team everyone wants to belong to? This reflection can help you identify the values you care most about and will further prompt your thinking on what type of leader you want to be.

My belief is at times when we find ourselves in uncomfortable positions wondering how we got there, in many instances we're in those positions because we didn't plan ahead on how we wanted to mold the situation. Because we go in with no plan, we end up being reactive instead of proactive.

The same happens when you begin as a team leader. When you have a clear understanding of your most cherished values, what type of leader you want to be, and how you would like your team to look like, you'll be in a much stronger position than if you just go into this new situation blindly.

TRANSITIONING TO TEAM LEADER

If, like Glenn at the beginning of the chapter, you're now leading colleagues who you used to be on the same level with, you may find your situation particularly tricky and fraught with stress. You may be worried about how you're going to maintain a friendship with these people. You may wonder how to avoid being seen as a big jerk, or on the other hand, ensure that people understand that now you are in charge and how to create adequate distance with your former colleagues, which did not use to exist.

The type of culture and organization you work in may also

influence how easy or hard this transition can be. In flat organizational structures or cultures, where people work in a highly-autonomous fashion, people might not give a second thought to your promotion. While in more hierarchical structures, your former colleagues might react more strongly. In this case, you can use a number of favourable strategies to make the transition easier for you, and hopefully, for your colleagues as well.

First, talk to each of your former team members at the office and have an honest and candid conversation about your new position. Listen to how they feel about it, what they are worried about, and so on. You don't need to offer solutions. Just show you're listening and considering what they say. If nothing else, this conversation will set a good example of constructive communication for the future.

Second, if you have true friends in the team you're going to lead, take time to meet with them outside of the office. You may want to discuss candidly each other's feelings and apprehensions about your new position. This exercise allows you to see you're not the only one who's worried about how this transition may affect your friendship, and many of your worries are mutual. After bringing everything out in the open, you and your friend can brainstorm strategies to make it work for both of you. Common strategies include:

- Maintaining a strict separation of personal and professional, i.e., personal issues are not discussed in the office and professional ones are not discussed outside the office.
- Agreeing to avoid arguments and confrontations of a professional (or personal) matter in front of other people at the office.
- Agreeing not to use your friendship status to gain advantages, favours, or favourite treatment, or, on the

other side, to be asked to stay late to complete projects or help out in other tasks.

- Agreeing about how you will deal with work parties and dinners to which one of you is not invited.

In our excitement about our new leadership position, we might forget to budget in the people around us, such as our co-workers who will now become part of our team. Acknowledging that the change is challenging not just for us but for them too is a great place to start ensuring a smooth transition. Dare to be the first to speak up and acknowledge uncomfortable situations. Most people will respect you and thank you for that.

DEFINING WHAT PROFESSIONALISM MEANS TO YOU

Another issue you may face when transitioning from team member to team leader is doubts as to whether some of your behaviours or routines as a team member are still what you want to project as a team leader. These doubts are linked to that vague term "professionalism."

The Merriam-Webster dictionary defines professionalism as *"the skill, good judgment, and polite behaviour that is expected from a person who is trained to do a job well."* But professionalism means different things to different people.

Inside the office, it may mean turning in your report before the deadline you promised. It may mean being in a meeting on time when you said you would be. It may mean doing your best work every time, no matter how tired you are or how mind-blowingly boring the task is. It may mean never raising your voice, being demeaning, or otherwise impolite to team members, colleagues, staff, and clients. It may mean not gossiping and limiting our complaining, whining, and other negative behaviours.

Take a moment to reflect on what professionalism means to you and whether you have certain behaviours you think might be important to tweak now that you're leading the team.

For example, while in the past complaining about boring tasks might've caused few problems, now it might backfire. Your complaining might signal to the team that it's OK for them to complain too, creating problems with team ambience and motivation. Also, while in the past you may have indulged in gossip about other team members or colleagues, as a leader it might be important to maintain impartiality and avoid any behaviours that people might interpret as you "siding" with one team member over another.

Another area to consider when thinking about professionalism is what happens outside of the office. What is adequate professional behaviour when you leave the office space and go out with your team for a beer, a celebration, or a retreat?

The internet has lots of advice, in blogs and in books, on what's considered as professional and what's not. However, different societies and organizational cultures have contrasting standards as to what is acceptable, and the ambiance in offices and companies can vary widely even within one country. What's important is you think ahead of time about these issues and come up with answers that suit your personality, that of your team and the organizational culture of your company and country.

Finally, also take the time to consider harassment issues. While harassment is a problem you have to consider whatever level you're at, things do change considerably when you're in a position of leadership. You're now responsible for ensuring a working ambience that promotes respect and strongly condemns harassment, including sexual harassment.

Whether men or women, as leaders we must strive to ensure a healthy, safe, harassment-free environment in our teams.

Remember that both men and women can harass and be harassed at work.

If you're not used to thinking about these issues, it is now important to educate yourself about them. Get to know your organization's policies on harassment, and start a respectful and honest discussion with your team. This can be key in establishing clear guidelines for all as well as a healthy working environment and signals to your team that it is OK to raise these issues with you.

* * *

Shifting from a team member to a team leadership position can be a bit of an upheaval. In the challenge and excitement of it, we might plunge in without much of a plan for handling the transition. In diving in like this we risk falling into uncomfortable and unexpected situations, which could have been prevented with a little proactive reflection.

This reflection includes determining what type of leader you want to be and what values you cherish. It also includes acknowledging that the change is challenging not just for you but for your colleagues and setting up a strategy to deal with this in a positive manner. Finally, it requires thinking about what you want to project as a leader, how to relate to your team members, and how to create a respectful working environment.

In the next chapter, we'll discuss traits and behaviours successful leaders have in common and strive to cultivate. These have to do with ways of thinking and how we relate to other people, our team members in particular. Some people call these "soft skills." Going back to Caroline Dweck's research on personal growth, we will use the term "mindset" to refer to them, to remind us that these traits can actually be changed and we can develop them in ourselves as we grow our teams.

Chapter 4
Your leadership mindset

Now that you have mapped out your skills and your influence zones and have identified the challenges you may face when transitioning from a team member to a team leader, it is time to take the next step and strengthen your leadership abilities. All of us, no matter what our natural skills and traits are, can with an appropriate growth mindset train ourselves to become better leaders.

In this chapter we will delve into common traits or skills that successful leaders share and that are normally cherished and prized by team members, and we'll discuss practical ways we can grow these attributes in ourselves. The list is by no means exhaustive, and is based on attributes I cherish the most. People may have differing views as to which traits are more important, and this will also depend on the environment you are in.

BE RESPONSIBLE

> *"The price of innocence is impotence. Be response-able."*
> *- Fred Kofman, VP at LinkedIn*[13]

In his book, *The 7 Habits of Highly Effective People*, Stephen Covey talks about "response-ability"--the ability to choose our own response. The thinking behind "response-ability" is that between any external stimulus and our response, rests our ability to choose. We do not simply react to the environment; we can choose how to respond.[14]

Accepting responsibility empowers us. When we blame the circumstances, conditions or our past, we may conveniently skirt the responsibility, but we also forsake our power. Without power it becomes that much more difficult to lead and to create great outcomes. Going back to our spheres of influence from Chapter 2, when you skirt responsibility, you are placing something in the outmost sphere: the far beyond, where you have no sway over it. When you accept responsibility, you are placing it in sphere one, your decision-making zone, where you have control over the outcome.

Stand up for your team

When it comes to leading your team, taking responsibility means when faced with external evaluation your team's successes are your team's successes but your team's failures are your own. Great leaders are quick to share the credit of triumphs with their teams and quicker to take the blame when something doesn't go as planned.

It doesn't matter if your team has screwed up big time and you're furious with them, when it comes to external parties, you stand up for your team. You defend the things they did right and take responsibility for the things that went wrong.

Taking responsibility isn't something you do only to maintain appearances or because you're expected to. It comes from a clear analysis of how this failure can be traced back to you and in what way you are responsible for it.

Every time something doesn't go as planned--your team misses a deadline or messes up an outcome--sit down and think hard about what went wrong. The easiest parts to identify are when a member of your team failed to do his or her duty. For instance, Jane doesn't review the editing of the report. Vishal fails to notice that the deadline has been moved. Kim forgets to return a client's call. Joy doesn't know how to solve a problem and fails to ask for help.

Now look beyond these issues. In every one of your team's failures or underperformances a part can be traced back to you. Find it. Ask yourself, what did I do or didn't do that allowed this to happen? Did I get in his or her way? Did I fail to request things on time? Knowing this person needs a lot of supervision, did I fail to provide it? Did I forget to review this in detail? Did I put too much trust on this person? Did I fail to manage the different team personalities in a constructive fashion?

The buck stops with you. At first, this idea may be hard to accept, and you may feel yourself rebelling against the notion and angry at your team for the failure. But taking responsibility is like exercising a muscle. The more you trace back the failures to you, the easier it becomes. In the end it'll become so automatic you'll think it is a reflex you've always had.

Owning up to your team's flops comes with many pluses. First, it's empowering. If the issue can be traced back to you, then it's in your power to solve it, to do a better job next time. You may not be able to change your team members, but by tracing the mistake back to you, you can definitely find ways to improve the outcomes. By taking responsibility, you're putting the issue squarely in your decision-making sphere, under your control.

Second, you'll have much less angst and stress. The blame-game is stressful. You have to have ugly confrontations with people. It's discouraging and tiring to see your team members blame each other. You'll get none of that when you own up to a mistake. You may feel some anguish at the idea of taking the blame but that will go away as soon as you step up and own it out loud.

Lastly, taking responsibility will do two powerful things to your relationship with your team: it will set a strong example and it will gain you their respect. We tend to respect individuals who take responsibility for their acts, particularly when we see a leader taking the blame for a team effort where more than one person made mistakes.

Move beyond blame

Responsibility is not only about owning up to a failure or mistake but also about moving beyond blame and towards solution-oriented thinking. When something goes wrong, it's important to sit down and reflect on what part of the responsibility can be traced back to you. This part you can change. But then it's time to let go of the mistake and look towards the future. How can you fix the current situation if that's still possible? If it is not possible to fix it, what lessons have you learned that will help you do better next time?

Identify also where members of your team could have done better. Make sure you have specific examples. Set up a meeting with your team and start by stating the failure or mistake and taking final responsibility for it. Then, ask each person to identify what he or she could have done better. Make it clear this is not about blaming others but identifying points of improvement in oneself.

Now focus your team on problem-solving, for either fixing the current situation or doing better next time. Ask everybody to contribute ideas and volunteer for tasks. In this way you can transform a failure into a team-building opportunity. Make sure you close the meeting with a strong plan and a team that's motivated to put it into practice.

Lead by example

If you want your team to step up and be responsible, make sure you set an example. Taking responsibility, acknowledging mistakes, showing persistence, maintaining calm in a crisis are all ways to set an example if you want to see more of these behaviours in your team.

Also, if you used to complain or whine when things went wrong, you don't have the luxury to do that anymore as a team leader. It pays to act as you would like each of your team members to act. If you want your team to be good-humoured in difficult times, you need to set the tone.

Rolling up your sleeves and pitching in with your team also shows responsibility and leadership and can gain you a lot of good will. Give a hand with particularly boring or repetitive tasks and with tasks where you have asked the whole team to contribute. Do you have to prepare a thousand envelopes in an afternoon to send out? Does your team need to work over a weekend to make the deadline for a proposal? Because of a mistake, does data need to be re-entered into the system before tomorrow morning? Stand by your team and pitch in. Set the example and show good humour and collaboration. Bring some brownies or beers and turn it into a fun work gathering.

BE DECISIVE

"In any moment of decision, the best thing you can do is the right thing, the next best thing is the wrong thing and the worst thing you can do is nothing."
- attributed to Theodore Roosevelt[15]

When I was an undergraduate student, I did some fieldwork in remote islands. One day we drove our little motorboat out to an isolated beach on the other side of the island from the living compound. While we were working on the beach, a storm broke out and the waves started getting higher and higher. Our little open motorboat was banked on the sand, and soon we wouldn't be able to push it back into the water past the breakers. Some of us had already started pushing the boat back into the water, but our team leader was undecided. Was it safer to stay on the beach and risk getting stranded here for a few days? Or was it safer to risk the waves and try to make it back to camp?

A shouting match ensued, with our leader demanding that we remain on the spot while he thought it through and me demanding that he made up his mind quickly because we needed to go. It wasn't until many weeks later, back in the normal city life, that I realized how much weight that decision had for him, as the safety of all of us rested in his hands, and how poorly I had supported him in that difficult decision moment.

In our normal work life, many of us never face decisions where other people's safety is at stake. But many of us have trouble with decision making. We may agonize over choices and fear making the wrong call.

Timely decision making is key to strong leadership. It allows your team to move forward fluidly and prevents frustration from building up due to unnecessary delays. Lengthy and unclear decision-making processes kill passion, motivation, and productivity. Too quick decision making, on the other hand, can also have negative effects, leading to failures or the need to redo or patch up work. Your team is working hard to make things happen. Your responsibility is keeping the momentum going by making the calls that need to be made at the appropriate time.

Just as important, timely decision making is good for you because every unmade decision is a dead weight around your neck, dragging you down and draining you. In this sense, indecision can be worse than the wrong decision. We all have limited amounts of energy. Make sure to put this energy into productive and creative use. Agonizing over decisions you are postponing leeches away at this precious energy.

While big, key decisions require thorough vetting of pros and cons, risks and consequences, and adequate time for discussion, reflection and gathering of information, the truth is that smaller, everyday decisions don't change outcomes that much. In any case, they don't change outcomes in a way that is significant enough for us to agonize over the decision.

Decision making is like a muscle. The more you exercise it the stronger it gets. If you are a person that has trouble with decision making, below are some ways to train your decision-making muscles and help you feel more confident about the process.

Start with small decisions

For two or three days, pay attention to every banal decision you make and make a list. You will see that most of these have no life-changing consequences, whatever you decide. For example, where you go for lunch or whether you choose to use the big or small meeting room.

Other decisions do have a small impact, but normally your choice will be between a good and a better choice. For example, you're trying to decide between using video or audio for your next advertising campaign or choosing one provider over another one. In these cases, it's not a big issue whether you "make the wrong call," as the wrong call will still be a solid, workable solution.

In other instances, your decisions can be reversed later on if time shows it wasn't the best solution, with minimal waste of time and resources. For example, you had prepared one poster design and you now wish to switch to another, but the posters haven't yet been printed.

Use these simple non-threatening decisions to exercise your decision-making muscle. Challenge yourself to be quick in deciding every day when you are presented with these choices so you help your team to maintain momentum.

Figure out what are you're waiting for

We can waver over decisions for more than one reason. Sometimes we're weighing the pros and cons or figuring out the risks of each choice. Other times we are trying to ensure everybody is in agreement and we can reach a consensus. We could also be waiting for more information. Being clear about why you're wavering can help make the call easier and set a strategy for moving forward.

For example, if you are trying to get everyone to agree, you can set up a strategy to foster consensus and set a deadline for when you will either go for a majority or, lacking that, make the call yourself.

If you are waiting for more information, figure out if you can actually get the information at some point and how long will it take. Try to imagine what this extra information would look like and how it would change your choice. Sometimes when we do this exercise we realize that this additional information, no matter what it says, won't change our choice. In which case, waiting is superfluous.

In some instances, you may realize what you are actually waiting for is for something or someone to make the decision for you. Realize this won't happen, go through a decision-making process (see below), and make the call.

Check for saturation

Saturation is a concept used in social science research to signify the moment in time when more research starts rendering redundant information.[16] At some point, while you're gathering information to make a decision, you'll notice the same evidence starts cropping up over and over again. This point can be reached when you are polling people for their opinions or gathering information from written sources.

When you reach saturation, further information-gathering or research is less likely to unearth anything truly new that could substantially alter the information you already have. At this point the balance tips and further information-gathering may become a waste of time. You've reached the moment of decision.

If participatory approaches are important for your decision making, double check you've listened to everyone's input and gathered opinions from all your team members and then make the call.

Try a decision-making model

There are many decision-making processes, from the simple but powerful pros and cons list to amazingly complex decision-making models. In the Notes and References section, I share some resources on decision-making models.[17] But don't add to your indecision by agonizing about choosing the right decision-making model!

Most decision-making models have at least three key steps in common: clarify the problem, gather information and search for alternatives, and analyse or compare alternatives. A clearer definition of the problem will facilitate the search for a solution. Looking for alternatives reminds us to think outside the dichotomy box (as discussed below). Analysing alternatives is what allows us to choose the one we think will bring the best results or aligns better with our goals or values.

The benefit of the models stems in no small part from the mental processes they trigger. You are creating the space and time to look at a decision in depth and following a step-by-step process, which reassures you that you have considered all angles and gathered all opinions. Processes help us systematize things, ensuring we think things through in a logical, organized manner and thus making it less likely that we've left out anything important.

Find the third way

One main issue with decision making is a common human bias which authors Dan and Chip Heath, in their New York Times bestseller book *Decisive*, refer to as the "spotlight effect,"[18] or what the Nobel prize winning psychologist Daniel Kahneman referred to as "what you see is all there is."[19] When we are making a decision, we normally only take into consideration the information right in front of us, forgetting to weight in the information not immediately available, which may be important to have.

The information presented to us in many cases looks like a choice between A and B. Using the Heath brother's "spotlight" metaphor, much as in a dark theatre, only choices A and B are in the spotlight and everything else disappears into the darkness. The problem is that the best solution may be just outside that circle of light, lurking in the shadows.

Imagine that Pune, one of your team members, tells you that Alex, a young volunteer at your organization, has not been doing a good job, has been arriving late, and has developed an annoying habit of distracting other volunteers while they're working by playing music. While Alex can work fast and efficiently when he wants to, Pune suggests that now is the time to say goodbye to Alex and asks for your opinion.

Immediately, you start weighing the pros and cons of letting Alex go or keeping him. The information presented by Pune--the one in the spotlight--is what is driving your mental process. Yet, there is a lot of information in the shadows you haven't even started considering. What are the reasons for Alex's late arrival? Maybe this has an easy solution? Is Alex demotivated in his work at your organization? Are the other volunteers truly distracted or annoyed by his music or is it just Pune? Is Pune's view of Alex accurate or is he somehow biased by a personal dislike of this volunteer? Between letting Alex go or keeping him are a myriad additional options: finding out how to motivate him or integrate him better, putting him under the charge of another team member, and so on.

As a leader, one of your greatest tools will be to think about what's not in the spotlight and provide alternative solutions to your team. If you manage to pull this off, you'll easily become the go-to person when someone is confronting a difficult choice.

What you want to develop is a "third-way reflex." Basically, you train your brain to automatically ask, "Is there a third option?", whenever anyone presents you with a supposedly binary alternative. In much the same way as your brain associates brushing your teeth with putting on your pyjamas, you want your brain to associate looking for a third option with any black or white choice you come across.

In the beginning, make sure to put up a big sticky note with the words "Is there a third way?" written on them, clearly visible on your desk or computer. In your meeting templates (see Chapter 7 and Clinic 17 in the Workbook), add a reminder at the end saying "Is there a third way?" Make sure you ask this question at any meeting where a decision is being made. Train yourself and your team to brainstorm all further possible solutions to a problem. Little by little, you will make a habit out of this, and you'll find that you immediately become suspicious when someone presents you with only two alternatives to a problem.

Decide not to decide

In some cases, after going through a decision-making process and considering third-way options, you'll realize you are truly not ready to make a decision. It's not fear of being wrong that is stopping you. You might be lacking information or need to consult other parties. You might be in a highly unstable or changing environment. Or you might even have realized that, for the time been, postponing this decision is the safest or smartest choice.

In this scenario, waiting is perfectly justifiable. It is important, however, to make it clear to yourself and to others that you *are* making a decision. You are deciding not to decide just yet. You have solid reasons for it, and thus, you'll be clearer on when a decision can be made, as you know what needs to change first.

Accept that you may be wrong

This is where exercising your responsibility bears fruit. The more you become comfortable with taking responsibility, the easier you'll find making decisions, since you'll feel comfortable owning up if you mess up. You know you can learn from your mistakes and start over. And most importantly, you know that making the call was best, despite the possibility of being wrong, and you did it.

BE HUMBLE

The man who was my boss for many years came from a tiny village in a rural area of Mexico, where there wasn't even a secondary school. He went on to study medicine in the capital and abroad. Eventually, he built up from nothing and against tremendous odds one of the most successful and compassionate clinics in the country for people living with HIV.

When I started working there, we weren't even thirty people. Two years later, our numbers had tripled. By the time I left, over 140 people worked there. Yet, my boss knew every single person's name. For the majority of them, he also knew the names of their partners and children.

The clinic stood inside a hospital with over three-thousand employees. When I walked with my boss to a meeting somewhere inside the hospital, I felt like I was walking with the president. He stopped every few meters to greet people, shake hands and ask them how they were doing. He knew the names of the directors and the cleaning crew people, the nurses and the doctors, the administrative assistants and the orderlies. Every morning he exchanged a friendly conversation with the guard at the entrance.

Patients loved him. He had patients and friends from all walks of life, from an illiterate woman in a rural village to an activist for ethnic minorities' rights, to media stars and powerful businesspeople. His power had made him many "enemies" too, who had done everything they could to stop the growth of his clinic and his dream. Yet, more than once I saw him receive calls from these "enemies" asking for medical help for a relative, and my boss was just as kind and compassionate with them as with anyone else.

To this day, I am still baffled by how long it took me to learn the clearest, most powerful lesson from this man--humbleness.

For a long time, the prevailing paradigm in work environments was that toughness and competitiveness were the way to go. To succeed you had to put yourself first. Leaders tended to emphasize their strength and competence.

That paradigm has been changing fast. In his book *Give and Take*, Adam Grant presents research showing that "givers," people who put others first and show humbleness and generosity in the workplace, actually "finish first". Grant compares "givers" to "takers," competitive types who put themselves first, and to "matchers," the "tit-for-tat" type who strive to preserve a balance between giving and taking, operating from a principle of fairness and reciprocating. Research shows that across a wide range of professions, "givers," provided they know how to set healthy limits, are more successful than "takers" or "matchers," in terms of productivity, effectiveness, and performance.[20]

Many of the traits that "givers" show have to do with humbleness: they take the time to learn people's names, they talk to everyone, and treat everyone kindly, not just powerful people who they want to connect with. They showcase other people's work and they promote the team's accomplishments before their own.

Amy Cuddy, from the Harvard Business School, along with other researchers, have shown that projecting warmth (communion or trustworthiness) can be as important or more for leadership than projecting competence and skill. This is because warmth facilitates trust and connection while projecting only competence can indeed lead to respect, but that respect might be laced with fear or mistrust.[21]

These researchers suggest that warmth can be shown by a host of behaviours, such as nonverbal signals of recognition--a nod, a smile, attention to people's concerns, and other signs that suggest you hear them and understand them.

Many of these behaviours have to do with humbleness, defined by the Merriam-Webster dictionary as "the absence of any feelings of being better than others." Acknowledging and recognizing others, making them feel visible, important and appreciated, being receptive and listening, and sharing credit are all linked to humility.

So what do humbleness and kindness look like in our everyday working life? How do we cultivate humbleness? As most everything else in this book, humility is a habit that we can acquire with practice. We start with the "small" things, which most people would find insignificant, and still build a strong base for trust.

Say, "Hi," to everyone

Every day, no matter your mood, make sure to greet everyone with a smile. From the doorkeeper to the CEO, everybody you cross gets a greeting from you, especially if they're in any way connected to your work. I'm amazed at how much we neglect or disregard the power of such a simple act. A greeting makes people feel *visible*. If you're now in a leadership position, recognizing people's visibility by greeting them is one of the strongest, easiest ways to create trust and mutual respect. Don't throw such a powerful tool out the window just because it seems so trivial.

Many of us tend to just go greet a person when we want something from him or her. Thus, we don't say hi to the receptionist unless we need to ask him to please send a visitor directly up to the office. We don't smile to the IT guy unless our computer is broken. This does nothing to build trust.

People will do what you ask them to do, but mostly because it's their job and they don't have an option. Not because they are happy to or feel any connection or loyalty to you. Without any connection, the result you get out of that person may not be their best effort.

Switch it around, say, "Hi," first. Start creating the basis for a trust system.

Greet all your team members, the cleaning person, the assistant, the intern, your colleagues from other departments. Some people might not say, "Hi," back. That's not your problem. Let go of your results. You'll still greet them warmly the next day. This is about you, not about them.

Make sure your boss, if you have one, also gets a greeting from you every day. We tend to forget that bosses are human beings like everyone else, and they'll also react positively to this. Don't go see them only when you need something from them. Include them in your greeting ritual.

Call people by their names

Just as greeting people is about visibility, so is recognizing and remembering their names. Dale Carnegie, in his all-time bestseller, *How to Win Friends and Influence People*, lists this as one of his key principles: "Remember that a person's name is to that person the sweetest and most important sound in any language."[22]

We are all egocentrics. It is part of what makes us human. It is flattering and agreeable when someone remembers our name. Just think about how you felt the last time someone forgot or mispronounced your name. Most of us tend to feel at least slightly annoyed.

Like me, you might realize that while you never forget a face, you have a terrible memory for names. For many years, I let this belief rule my life. It became a very convenient excuse for not trying harder to remember people's names.

Then I noticed the small changes that happened when instead of just saying, "Hi," I said "Hi, Lisa" or "Hi, Pablo." People perked up. They seemed genuinely pleased. They said, "Hi," back. They started greeting me first in the hallway. They were more open when I asked for something, and they even started coming to me to share information.

I embarked on a campaign to learn two new names per week. The more names I learned, the easier it became to learn them.

Actually, the hardest part turned out to be asking the names of people that I had been crossing in the hallway for months and months. I was quite embarrassed to admit that I didn't know their names!

Start small. Go for one or two names per week. If you have a really bad memory for names, look up mnemonic techniques to help you remember them. Repeating the name back to the person when you meet them is a good strategy, as is repeating the name silently three times in your head. Quiz yourself an hour later or at the end of the day to see if you remember it. Write it down as soon as you are out of sight of the person.

Like in my experience, the hardest part may well be admitting your ignorance of people's names. Don't let this deter you. Say, "I'm so sorry. My memory is terrible. Would you remind me of your name?" If you can't bring yourself to ask the person directly, ask around or use the company directory.

In Clinic 6 in the Workbook you will find some small experiments you can do to learn new names and start greeting people more often.

Share the credit

Great leaders are not only quick to accept the blame, as we have seen, they are also quick to share the credit. In many instances, you will be representing your team while they're not there. It would be easy to forget to mention them and, instead, implicitly or explicitly take ownership of their successes.

Don't give in to this temptation. Make sure every time you're presenting you share the credit and call out individual contributions and achievements.

In many projects, your team will have those more visible people who are in charge of programs, projects, design, implementation, as well as the less visible people on the back end who silently keep everything running smoothly. Typically, the first group gets recognized often, while the second, in many cases, gets ignored. But their work is key.

The administrative staff, IT and web programmers, financial staff, drivers, receptionists, and others are the ones who provide the infrastructure on which everything else rests. But because their contributions are harder to trace to a specific accomplishment or outcome, they're normally overlooked. Pay special attention to this, and make sure to acknowledge these team members as well. Because in many cases they're used to being overlooked, you might be surprised at how much good will you can foster by acknowledging their work publicly.

Share the credit with all your team members both in presentations and big meetings and also privately in small-talk when you discuss projects with bosses, directors, colleagues and so on. News travels fast in most office settings and privately sharing credit will gain you the respect and trust of your team and also build good will and foster collaboration.

BE CARING

"Care about your people as people."[23]

I used to believe professionalism meant personal things weren't discussed on the job. I was wrong. Some people are better than others at leaving their personal issues at the door when they come to the office, but in truth what happens on one side of our lives affects the other and vice versa.

Thus, as a team leader, you cannot simply ignore your team's personal lives or demand a strict work-life separation. On the contrary, you can gain much by caring about your team members' lives.

If, when we talk to our team members, we are only concerned with work-related issues, the depth of communication and trust we create will only go so far. Also, we'll miss out on key information that could help us understand poor performance, demotivation, and burnout.

Caring for your people as people means caring for them beyond the workplace too. It is about seeing them as human beings with friends, families, dreams, and worries. Not just as pieces of your organization's machinery.

We care about people because it aligns with our values.

Because we believe we should treat our team members as we would like to be treated.

Caring about your people also makes sense for business. Businesses with engaged employees tend to outperform those with disengaged employees,[24] and one consistent key driver of engagement seems to be the relationship with the immediate supervisor.[25]

Data suggests that a good relationship with a team leader or manager stems from several factors. One is focusing on individual's strengths: engagement is 61% in teams whose managers concentrate on their employee's strengths but 45% in those whose managers concentrate on weaknesses, and it plummets to 2% in managers who ignore their teams.[26]

Another is caring about your people: a survey among American workers showed that 54% of employees who believed their managers cared about them personally are engaged, compared to only 17% of those who don't think their managers care about them as people.[27]

There are several strategies you can use to show kindness and caring.

Ask about their lives

A great way of getting to know your team is making sure you take some time to chat. Chatting usually feels like a waste of time, but it can be an investment. It helps you to get to know your team better, allowing you to be better positioned when conflict or overwhelm arise.

Ask your team about their families, their hobbies, what did they do on the weekend or on vacation time. Ask about their dreams and favourite foods and their new car and the sports team they support.

Make a point of following up on things they shared with you. This shows that you didn't just ask out of politeness but true interest. If their child is sick, remember to ask the following day how he or she is doing. If they went on vacation, remember to ask how the beach was. If their soccer team played last night, ensure you discuss the score.

This will show them that you care about them not only as resources to the organization's goals but also as human beings. It's about connection. The more threads connecting you with your team, the stronger the bonds. Stronger bonds create trust and will give people more reason to do their best and enjoy their work.

Think about how you would like to be treated

Years ago, when my grandmother passed away, I was scheduled to leave for an important conference. I decided to cancel my attendance in order to fly to my grandmother's home country and be with my family. My boss at the time was not happy with my decision, and tried to dissuade me. Although he accepted it in the end, I would've really appreciated a lot more support from him at such a trying time.

We've all been there at some point. Receiving bad news while at work. Having an unexpected family issue clash with an important job matter. Anguishing over missing your child's school festival or looking bad at work for going. Think beforehand about the situations that may arrive with your team and how would you like to be treated if you were in their place.

If you've created enough trust, chances are that, when such a situation arises, your team members will feel comfortable confiding in you. When this happens, do your best to support them. Listen to their issue. Help them in negotiating with the organization or HR. Support them with figuring out how everybody can pitch in to cover for them.

Care about their professional wellbeing

Caring for your team also means seeing to their professional well-being. Ensure you have strategies in place for preventing burnout. Check in regularly to see if your team members are motivated, getting enough feedback, and doing work they find meaningful. If they want to continue their professional development, support them in negotiating with the organization. If they've been doing great work, make sure you highlight their accomplishments inside and outside the organization. Support them for promotions, training and other benefits. Make sure they're taken into consideration in decisions and their voices are heard.

In Clinic 7 in the Workbook you'll find one exercise you can do to figure out how much you know and ignore about your team members and set yourself on the path to knowing them better.

BE A MENTOR

One day Gina, one of my best team members, came to me and told me flatly: "We need to talk about Ulf. This isn't working anymore." Ulf was one of my team members. But he worked partly under her responsibility.

For the past year and a half, as Ulf's work quality and motivation had taken a decidedly downwards turn, I had twice suggested to Gina that we might consider letting him go and finding a replacement. Gina had stood up for him. We'd only kept him onboard because Gina defended him. She was convinced he would manage to turn it around and she had been providing support for that. But now she was done. She was overwhelmed and she was feeling burned out.

I had to act. However, when the possibility of letting go of Ulf finally opened up, I wavered. On one side, I was conscious we could possibly find someone much better if we took the risk and let Ulf go. On the other side, I knew he'd been a great worker at some point. The downturn had come after a difficult event in his personal life.

When I sat down to make an objective list of pros and cons, I realized that while the con list was longer and much of his record in the past months was dismal, the pros were powerful ones.

Our main aim at the organization was always our beneficiaries' well-being. Everything was measured based on that yardstick. And on that one his performance was impeccable. Beneficiaries loved him. He was kind and patient and always had time for them.

I decided to extend him a the three-month trial period for turning things around if he truly wanted it. And in those three months, I would commit to mentoring him intensely. I would remove Gina from the responsibility of dealing with his shortcomings and would take that upon myself.

I talked with Gina. She thought this was a fair solution that made her immediately feel better and took a weight off her shoulders. In a sense, the final responsibility of deciding his fate in the organization would now fall on me.

So I started my experiment. First, I talked to Ulf and explained that things were not working out and told him truthfully that we were considering letting him go.

But I also explored his motivation to stay by asking one question: "Maybe this job isn't a good fit for you anymore. Maybe it's boring. Or you've grown out of it and now have other interests. Have you ever thought about whether there's something else that you'd rather be doing?" I told him he could think about that for a few days and then we could talk some more.

We met up again after a few days, and he told me this was really what he wanted to do. He wanted to stay. So we fleshed out a plan. I explained he would have all the support he needed and the majority of that support would come directly from me. I shared with him my list of his pros, of all the things he did well and all the potential I saw in him.

We planned weekly accountability meetings and a set of clearly defined goals. His first goal was to get the professional help he needed to deal with his personal issues.

Four weeks later, I met with Gina to get her opinion on how things were going. She was pleasantly surprised. Ulf had staged an amazing turnaround. She no longer had to cover up for him or complete or correct his tasks. He had become much more proactive in coming up to her to ask for support or tell her about problems. We even heard outside proof of how he was standing up more for himself and for the beneficiaries.

He had started using calendars and agendas and other time-planning tools, and proactively telling Gina when he thought she was pushing too hard. He'd been on time for his meetings with me every week and had come prepared with his set of goals and achievement status.

At the three-month mark, I talked to him again and told him we were thrilled with his turnaround. We definitely weren't going to let him go, unless of course he wanted to. Since the feedback system had worked, we'd maintain it and have an evaluation at six months and a year.

He thanked me for believing in him. Believing in him wasn't that big of a deal for me. I'd done my homework. I knew if he managed to turn it around, this would be a win-win for all: for our beneficiaries, for me for not having to go through the painful process of firing him and laboriously hiring of someone new, and for the team, because of his creativity, wit, and good humour. But my belief in him was important for him. He reasoned that even if he couldn't see it yet himself, I had to have a good reason for rooting for him, and he held on to that.

To be clear, I'm not advocating always keeping people who are not performing up to the required standard. Sometimes it is necessary to let go of people, and in many organizations we won't have the time or support from above to give people a second chance. What I'm advocating for is mentoring.

For me, this situation with Ulf was the plainest example of what mentoring can do for someone. Mentoring is a powerful tool, which stems from a strong belief in your team members. A belief that's easy enough to have if you cultivate a growth mindset.

Mentoring your junior team members will be one of the smartest time investments you make. Growing your people has positive repercussions all around. You team member will gain a lot, you will learn and be challenged, and the organization and team will benefit through better performance and results.

Mentoring does not have to be a costly time commitment. It can be an hour per month or half an hour per week. Consistency is key, however. You and your mentee have to commit to meeting regularly and come to that meeting well-prepared.

To set up a mentoring process with one of your team members, start with a first meeting to discuss overall mentoring goals. Figure out what challenges they're experiencing and what areas they want to grow in. Discuss how this mentorship relation can help your team member to build new skills, explore new ideas, expand their network, build their confidence, or even forge a new career path.

Then agree on the top three goals to focus on for now. For those three goals, detail an action plan, which may include responsibilities and commitments from you and your mentee, a meeting schedule (when, where, how often and for how long you're going to meet), and any confidentiality issues important for each of you.

Maintain momentum by showing up to subsequent meetings and sticking to your commitments. Come prepared with notes on the progress you have observed and any actions you took on your side as agreed. Also, make sure the other person shows up with clear notes on progress, stumbling blocks, and potential solutions for moving forward you can discuss together.

Let's say that after listening to your mentee, Rick, you realize he's getting bored with his current admin tasks, and he has a keen interest and good skills for finances. After you hear him out, brainstorm creative ways together to link those interests with the organization's interests. You might find a possibility for him to have more financial responsibilities in the organization. But he might require some training, which you can't provide. Determine the areas where you *can* provide support and help him brainstorm ways to get the training he needs.

Plan out your next mentoring meeting and determine what both of you will do between now and then. For example, Rick will find out what workshops are available on financial administration and you'll look up whether the organization could support him financially or with time availability or maybe both. You could both commit to discuss potential career changes within the organization with HR or leadership.

* * *

Your leadership soft skills fall into two categories: the first set is about your own empowerment. About making the mental shift that lets you step up by being responsible and decisive.

In the second category are the skills that help you connect with people at work, particularly with your team members. Research has shown that being humble, kind, and considerate is a winning strategy in the 21st century workplace and makes sense for business. Developing these qualities starts with the small things, like making people feel visible and ensuring they know you care for them not only as assets for the organization but also as human beings.

Your leadership skills are one side of the coin. They will create an environment of trust and mutual accountability and collaboration. But being responsible, decisive, and caring will only take you so far. Leaders get things done. They show results. And to achieve results you need sound organizational and time management strategies. We'll look into these in the next chapters.

CHAPTER 5
YOUR PLANNING STRATEGIES

WHILE leaders in different businesses and organizations will have differing skills specific to their areas, they will still have two things in common: a leadership mindset, which we discussed in the previous chapter and strong leadership strategies for *getting things done*. These strategies are based on good planning and time management skills.

In this chapter, we'll cover basic organizational and planning strategies and, in the next one, we'll delve into time management strategies. You'll be able to apply these immediately in your new leadership position.

First, we will tackle being overwhelmed, a recurrent feeling when we start in a new leadership position. I'll share a simple tool you can use every time you feel like your plate is too full and you are overstretched. Then we'll dive into long-term planning skills: how to set strong goals and how to plan for your year, your quarter and your month.

If you are feeling completely overwhelmed and on the edge of an impending burnout, start straight away with the section below on regaining control of your week. You can move on to the next sections on long-term planning later. Trying to go into long-term planning now will just increase your stress levels.

If you are feeling in control in the short term but are having trouble with clarity for the future and long-term planning, skip the next section and start reading the section about SMART objectives.

REGAINING CONTROL OF YOUR WEEK

Do you feel like you have too much to do? Does your brain feel like a beehive buzzing with ideas and worries clamouring for your attention? Every time you sit down to work on something do you get stumped because you can't figure out which priority to tackle first? Is your to-do list so long that just seeing it creates anxiety? If so, you may want to do this easy exercise first so you can regain a feeling of control over your activities.

Grab a piece of paper, the bigger the better, and crayons or markers in different colours. Shut the door to your office, lock yourself in the bathroom, escape to the rooftop, or otherwise make sure you'll be alone for the next thirty minutes. In Clinic 8 in the Workbook, you will find a template, which you can use as a guideline for this exercise.

Put it on paper. Grab a black marker and no particular order or logic, write down in black marker every single thing floating around in your mind and pestering you: meetings, deadlines, reports, activities, delays, worries about a specific team member, feelings of inadequacy, forgetting to feed the dog, your quarrel with your partner, the annoying flickering light bulb that needs to be replaced, the ticket planes you haven't yet bought, the little voice that is saying "you won´t make it," the pile of unanswered email, and so on.

You get the idea. You want it *all* out there: personal and professional, big and small, even if it sounds irrelevant or ridiculous. No one will see this piece of paper but you, and you can burn it afterwards if you want, so just get it all out. Don't stop or think about it. Don't try to order it or categorize it, just empty your brain of all the things buzzing inside it.

Once you feel it is all out, stop, take a breath and take a step back. Normally just getting it all out there on paper will provide some relief. This is because you were using your brain for storage. The more we use it for storage of things to do and things to worry about, the less it works for actually getting those things done. Now that you've transferred all this to a piece of paper, you can stop worrying about forgetting some key thing you need to do, and you can focus on getting things done.

Categorise it. The second step is to sort through the mess. Here's where your colour markers come in. First, you clean up the trash. Choose a specific colour marker for the trash, say brown. Circle anything that fits the trash category. You send to the trash *anything over which you have no control*. This includes things you're worrying about for which worrying serves no constructive purpose.

Go back to your influence spheres that you mapped out in Chapter 2. Anything that seems to belong to the third and last sphere of the far beyond gets circled in brown. If you can't change it and it's not in your influence zone, worrying about it won't change a thing. Recognize it and then let it go. Put it in the "trash."

Are you worrying about the potential merger? You have no control over it, so that goes in the trash. Worrying about what your team members are saying about you? None of your business. Circle it in brown and trash it too.

For items that you think you might be able to influence but need more time to sort through, choose another colour, say purple, for a "file for later" category.

Then create more practical categories to sort through your remaining stuff: e.g., personal, admin, program content, implementation issues, marketing, management and leadership, team issues, planning and strategy, and such. Choose a colour for each category and start circling items related to these different categories in the appropriate colour. By the end of your exercise, everything should be circled in a different colour.

This exercise works for two main reasons. First, because you empty your brain of everything buzzing inside it on paper, so the underlying worry of forgetting something disappears. Second, because you compartmentalize the stuff in your brain. Compartments or categories create order and order helps us feel in control. Getting you back in control is the point of this exercise.

Make space. Next, we will make room in your calendar this week by moving things over to next week and by delegating. Grab your black marker again. Start marking with a "NW" (Next Week) every item that can wait until next week or later. (Yes, there *are* items on that paper that can wait until next week. Go and find them.) For each item, ask yourself: will everything collapse this week if I don't get this one accomplished? If the answer is no, then put a "NW" on it.

Delegate. Now think hard about what you can delegate. If you think there isn't anything you can delegate, go take a peek at the last section in this chapter, entitled "Delegating," and then come back to this. Any item that looks suspiciously admin-related needs to be delegated to your assistant if you have one. Any issue not a hard-core competency of yours would be better in the hands of someone with stronger specific skills. Write a big "D" in front of all items you can delegate.

Prioritise. You are almost done now. The next step is prioritising what still remains on the list, that is every item not circled in brown (trash) or the file for later category, and not marked with an "NW" or a "D."

Of these remaining items, which are your most important priorities? If you are having a hard time figuring this out, ask, "If everything breaks down and I can get only one of these items done this week, which one would it be?" Write a number 1 on your first priority. Then ask the question again for the remaining ones, and write a number 2 on the second and so on until all of them get a number.

Now it's time for reality checks. How long will each of these priority items take? Try to estimate a number of hours for each of them. Remember to add a little buffering time. If they are not result-bound (i.e., "finish the report for the donor"), make sure you time-bound them (e.g., research service providers for 2 hours").

Calendarise it. Finally, get out your calendar for this week. Start by roping off time for all events that are already booked: non-negotiable meetings, appointments with clients, and so on. Then reserve time for your most important priority at the time of day where you are most effective, or as your first item for the day. Research has shown that doing our most important priority first thing in the day can have benefits, as we still have all our will power. Most of the things that we schedule to do in first thing in the day *do get done*, while many things we leave for later in the day will get postponed. Continue scheduling your priorities from number one to the last one, using progressively less efficient times of the week.

Hopefully, in the end you'll see that, if you keep to your schedule, everything will fit in. You may even have some room to breathe. Now you have a strong plan to get back in control. Go act on your plan.

SMART GOAL-SETTING

SMART stands for Specific, Measurable, Attainable, Relevant and Timely (or Time-Bound) goals. As the SMART acronym has proliferated, different words have been linked to each letter, so you'll find variants of what the acronym actually stands for. Also, probably due to its proliferation, the value and power of the acronym has seemed to fade, if only because of overuse and misuse. Still, SMART goal-setting is one of the greatest tools in your arsenal for reaching your goals.

SMART goals need not be complicated. In fact, they're very common sense, and you probably, in one way or another, already follow one or more of the letters in this acronym when you're setting your goals.

Let's work through the acronym with an example. Say that the big yearly goal for your team is developing a workshop. This is your WHAT.

S=Specific. In order for it to be **Specific**, you need to add more information to this goal: what the workshop is about, who you're selling it to, where it will happen. A specific goal would be "developing and selling a workshop on healthy eating to college students in our city."

Specificity highlights that this goal has various parts that need to come together, sequentially or in parallel, to get achieved. First, you need to design the workshop, then you need to create the materials, pilot it, develop the marketing material (website, flyers, emails, Facebook ads, tweets, etc.), set up a registration page, prepare a launch, plan the event, and so much more.

M=Measurable. To add the M for **Measurable**, answer the question "How will I know when my goal is accomplished?" Is it accomplished if you sell one unit of the workshop? Probably not. Let's say then that you'll sell a thousand spots of the workshop.

A=Attainable. I like to look at the A for **Attainable**, as the reality check of the M. Can M be attainable in the time frame of this year? Can you sell a thousand spots of the workshop if your list of contacts is around five hundred? Maybe not. So you may want to cut down on your goal and agree to sell two hundred spots or reach two hundred attendees if your workshop is for free. Attainable is what reminds us to look over our resources and our team's other commitments and obligations to ensure the goal is realistic and achievable in a set period of time.

R=Relevant. Being **Relevant** means this goal of creating a workshop is in line with the rest of your team's and organization's goals. This workshop could bring in more clients. It could mean more sales of your company's other products. Or if you're a not-for-profit, it could follow your organization's goal of promoting healthy eating habits among young people.

But it could also be the product of someone's wild imagination without adding value to the organization's bottom line. It may also be extremely important but not inside the boundaries of what your team is tasked to achieve, so not relevant for your team per se, while relevant for the larger organization. Checking your R is about taking a step back and asking if this is the best use of your and your team's time and resources.

T=Time-bound. Finally, the T is for **Timely or Time-bound**. I call this the double deadline. One deadline is the attainment of the numeric goal (e.g., two hundred units of the workshop sold), the other of the time-frame goal, e.g., we will sell two hundred units by June 1st this year. Be sure you use the A (Attainable) to do a reality check on T as well. Is June 1st attainable with your current resources and in view of your other commitments?

More nebulous goals can also greatly benefit from being time-bound. For example, you need to research the material for a new book or article. You have no idea how much material is out there so you have no clue how much time researching will take. To contain this goal, you can use the time-bound approach: I will research the book material for three hours, two times a week on Wednesday and Friday evenings. This way you know that when you've done six hours of research in a week, you've accomplished the goal.

SMART goal setting is important for completing tasks. Completion is key for progress, but it is also extremely important for *motivation*. You can't complete nebulous goals because you can't say when you've achieved them. With a SMART goal, you'll know for sure when you've reached the finish line. Then you can go out for dinner to celebrate, take the team out for beers, or throw an office party.

The sense of completion is powerful. The more we complete, the more capable we feel, and thus the more things we want to complete. If ever you're feeling demotivated, look into your goals. When's the last time you knew for sure you'd completed a goal and stopped to celebrate that accomplishment properly?

PLANNING WITH THE END IN MIND

Years ago, I was asked to coach a PhD student in the lab where I worked. She was smart and hard-working, but the head of the lab was worried because she wasn't getting enough results. I observed her for a while and couldn't find anything wrong in her techniques or scientific reasoning.

Then one day I noticed she was launching an experiment that would be finished two months from now, at a date I had already booked--for my own work--the machine she would need to read her results. Talking to her about this, I realized this was a recurrent issue.

The problem laid in her planning skills. The complex experiments she was doing required planning over long periods of time. But she was starting her experiments without this prior planning, resulting in reagents missing or equipment not being available at key points. I then remembered how I had the same problem when I was a first-year graduate student until a fantastic, hyper-efficient lab technician had shared her planning tricks with me.

I sat down with my student with a big calendar and a marker and showed her how I did my own planning. I started from the date when the machine had slots available to read my results and then worked backwards to identify the dates where I would need other equipment or new reagents or to perform intermediate steps. All the way back to the date where it was best to start my experiment. She got the hang of it quickly. Some months later, she had amassed an impressive collection of results.

Planning skills are key in all projects and, in particular, for complex projects with several players. Architects need them when building a house to ensure all the materials are ordered and delivered at the right times. They also need them to coordinate with the teams that need those materials: construction crews, carpenters, painters, and so on.

Healthcare workers need them to ensure medicines and supplies are available at all times, that surgery theatres and hospital beds are made ready and occupied in the most efficient fashion. Educators, scientists, writers, designers and more also need them. Yet, many non-administrative, non-managerial careers don't teach planning and project management skills to students. Many of us are left to learn them on the spot at our jobs.

In the following pages we'll look into some of these planning skills. We'll start with deadline-based planning, the type I taught my student. (Also called retro-planning or reverse planning.) Here you start from the deadline date and work it out backwards to today's date. This helps you to see more clearly when each milestone needs to be done so that the goal is completed by the deadline.

Retro-planning works best for goals with a set deadline, such as events. It can also help you think logically through other goals that are more cumulative in nature (e.g., sales, consultations, etc).

Let's imagine your goal is an event: you're going to organize a one-day event with some of the most renowned speakers in your area of work. Because June 1st is an important date in your profession, you've decided to plan the event for that date. How do you get there? How do you ensure that everything happens in time?

Start by getting a computer or paper-based calendar and mark your deadline in it. In this case June 1st. Now we start counting backwards from there.

Think about the limiting factors. These are factors outside of your control that could endanger your event if you didn't look into them in time. Even if you spend the whole week before the deadline cramming to make them happen, the goal still wouldn't be achieved.

In our example, because you've committed to a very specific date, the first limiting factor would be the venue. You know conference venues get pretty full at that time of year, so you need to book it well in advance. You want to make sure you've decided on it by March 1st. Note this date down in your calendar.

Now ask what needs to happen before this date in order to reach this milestone. What needs to happen before March 1st in order to secure the venue? Well, possibly you and your team need to look up venues online, call them to check availability, make a pre-selection, and go visit a small number of them before making the final call. All this needs to happen before March 1st!

Work it backwards. The pre-selection visits need to be completed by February 21st so you have a week to discuss the final decision and book the venue, which means you can use the week from the 14th to the 21st of February to go visit your top three selections. Thus, by the 14th of February you need to have set up all visits, so you can use the first two weeks of February to browse venues online and make the calls.

Another limiting factor may be the speakers. If you are

committed to get certain speakers for the event, you need to ensure they're available early on. Follow a similar procedure as for the venue. Mark the dates for when you need to have final confirmation, the dates when you need to send invitation emails or calls, and dates for reminders.

Plan what you have control over. You've settled the limiting factors, so you can start planning what needs to happen around these but which you have more control over. Make a list of everything you need to prepare and schedule: advertising, content, meals, travels, hotels, and so on. Then go down that list thinking about when each of the items needs to take place.

For example, let's say you want to do an intensive six-week advertising campaign right before the event. This means that by April 15th all advertising materials need to be ready. If you think creating the materials will take three weeks, you'd better start to work on these nine weeks before June 1st.

Then the programme contents need to be completed *before* the development of advertising materials. That will take four weeks, which means they need to be started, at the latest, thirteen weeks before June 1st.

You get the idea. Make sure you go down the list and include them all in your retro-planning calendar.

Think about your resources and factor in how these affect your retro-planning. For example, if the person who creates the programme is different from the one responsible for the marketing, some overlap between these two activities might happen. Could you complete the programme and tweak it while the marketing materials are being developed? Could you work on setting up the event (booking the venue, making the programmes, etc.) while the advertising campaign is ongoing?

As always, two pairs of eyes are better than one, so brainstorm your retro-planning calendar with some members of your team or discuss it in a team meeting. By the end of the exercise, you'll have a clearly marked retro-planning calendar, where it is obvious what each person needs to get done and by which date, in order for the event to be a success. Now share the calendar online with your team and put it up where everyone can see it.[28]

FROM BIG TO SMALL

Now that you have a tool for creating individual SMART goals and planning with an end goal in mind, we need to look into the big picture and drill down from there. The big picture could be your yearly goals; although, you might even have a three- or five-year vision. If your environment is too changing or unstable, your big picture, on the other hand, might be three months or less. Here we'll start with the yearly process that drives many organizations, but you can adapt this to your own needs.

You can do your planning on several available free or paid planning tools online or you can use a simple spreadsheet. Whatever system you choose doesn't need to be fancy. It just needs to be practical *for you*. And it should be user-friendly and provide a clear overview. You can even plan on a big piece of paper pinned to your office wall or on a whiteboard.

Yearly planning

The importance of yearly planning is that it identifies proactively what goals you want to accomplish, and it forces you to think about how to get to them. It also sheds light on whether the goals are feasible with your current resources and which times of the year might get hectic. This allows you to plan in advance for when you might need reinforcements or for times when people might be asked not to leave for holidays. In the hospital where I used to work, for instance, we knew that right after Christmas holidays there was a big influx of patients, so people were asked not to leave on vacation during January.

Clinic 9 in the Workbook has a table that you can use for your yearly planning and further tweak to your own needs, along with an exercise sheet summarising what we'll discuss below.

Write down your goals. Start with the yearly goals of your company; add your own professional goals and the ones for your team. Check to see that your yearly goals are SMART. If not, start by making them so.

Type of goal. Take your first goal and think about the type of goal this is. Is it a one-off event like a conference or a fundraiser dinner? Is it, on the contrary, a goal you'll get to by attaining smaller milestones along the year? For example, selling a specific number of items or covering a certain number of beneficiaries or clients? Is it a growing creative project such as a book or manual, a house renovation, or an educational project?

In the first case, the **"one-off goal,"** your activities will build up towards that goal, possibly getting more hectic the closer you get to the deadline.

For the second, the **"additive goal"** you might gain more out of maintaining an even distribution of smaller milestones throughout the year. Additive goals can combine regular strategies with single time-point strategies such as launches, promotional events, campaigns, or fairs to ensure you bulk up your numbers or make up for any shortcomings and hit your target.

For the third, the **"creative/growing goal,"** you need regular milestones to show progress. These types of projects may evolve over time. So you can also use those milestone points to decide on any change in course.

Action steps. Now, for each goal, think of the logical steps needed for your team to achieve that goal. Write down those logical steps. Remember this is the big picture. You're using a yearly framework so your action steps don't need to be very detailed. Broad action steps work well.

For example, for "Conference," you could write down: choosing a date, choosing a venue, preparing a program, preparing marketing materials, etc. You'll have an opportunity to details these further in your quarterly planning.

Timeframe. Now think of the time of the year when you'll have to take care of this particular action step. If the goal is the annual company's event that happens every 1st of October and the planning for that event takes three months, then you know the planning will occupy your third trimester (Q3, third quarter of the year, from July to September). This way when you come down to your quarterly planning, you will know which action steps you need to further deconstruct and detail for each quarter.

Milestones. Think of how you'll know when that particular action step is accomplished. This is your milestone. For example, for choosing a venue for the event, the end goal is not only to choose a venue but to actually go on and reserve it. Write down your milestone for each action step. For add-up milestones, this could be the number of sales or patients seen that you would like to achieve in that particular time period. For creative projects, it can be a partial step such as completing two chapters of the book, having a demo or pilot ready, and so on.

Deadlines. Now start your retro-planning. Grab your calendar and mark the final deadline for the goal. Start working backwards to set deadlines for each milestone. For this goal, and seeing all the logical steps, when does each step need to be finalized in order to achieve the final deadline? While for one-off or creative goals you might have specific deadlines, for add-up goals, your deadline might just be the last day of the month when you want to have reached that sales milestone, for instance.

Person in charge. Now decide which person of your team will take charge of that particular piece of the puzzle or action step, and write it down in too. This doesn't mean that this person has to do all the work, just that she is responsible for getting everyone to work together to accomplish the milestone in time. This is the person you'll be checking in with for that action step.

If you see your name too often in that last column, you might need to improve your delegating skills. Your job as a team leader is to ensure all of these steps happen effectively and are woven together to achieve your final goals, as well as to provide the support your team members need to accomplish this. You can't do this well if you're also doing most of the tasks! Imagine what would happen in a concert if an orchestra director was trying to play the violin at the same time as he directed and you'll get the picture.

Go through this same process for each of your goals. By the end you should have a pretty good idea of what needs to happen, when it needs to happen, and whose responsibility it is to make it happen.

Factor in delays. Make sure you leave a buffer between the completion of a step and the beginning of another one, in case there are delays. Delays are part of life. You can't control every variable, so delays *will* happen. Don't try to ignore them. Instead, plan for them, ensuring they don't shatter your schedule.

In the software developer world, most people acknowledge figuring out the precise amount of time needed to develop a program is difficult. That's because while you may have a general knowledge of how the program should be developed, you're bound to hit snags about things that you had no way of foreseeing. As a result, some developers calculate the time they *think* they'll need to complete the task and then multiply it by Pi. (Pi, a hazy memory from high school for most of us, is a mathematical constant that you obtain when you divide any circle's circumference by its diameter and is rounded to 3.14.)

While triplicating your time estimate may be too much in your situation, make sure you have at least a couple of days if not a week here and there between milestones, to buffer the delays that will surely come up.

Quarterly planning

Now that you have the big picture covered, you'll zoom in by creating ninety-day plans. Your quarters could be January-March, April-June, July-September and October-December, but they could also be any ninety-day period that works for you. For example, school years normally start in August or September and fiscal years in April or May. Adjust your quarters to your own situation.

First, take your calendar and mark off a whole morning at the end of each quarter. For example, on the last Friday of December, March, June, and September. Use these times to do your quarterly planning. Make sure you have alarms and other reminders set up so you remember these times.

Now concentrate on your first quarter. In your calendar, start by marking vacation time for each of your team members and yourself, as well as any holidays. Then add any non-negotiable items such as board meetings, meetings with your boss, HR, networking events, and others.

This process is an eye-opener. We think we have twelve weeks per trimester, but after this exercise it might look more like nine to ten weeks when accounting for everyone's vacation time and holidays, company meetings, and other non-negotiable items. And your planning has to be adjusted accordingly.

Now that you've done this reality check, take your goals and activities for the first quarter from your yearly plan and dissect them some more.

Determine the logical action steps for each goal. Repeat the process you did for the yearly goals but at a finer detail level. For example, think what needs to happen in order to "prepare the program for the conference." You probably need to come up with a proposed list of invited speakers, then check which of them are available and willing to participate, then determine the titles and order of the talks, lunch pauses, networking time, and so on. And finally hire a designer, format and print the program.

Add your milestones and deadlines and put a person in charge of that particular sub-task, if appropriate. Remember to leave in some buffer for delays.

Monthly planning

While you're doing your quarterly planning, rope off one or two hours of the last working morning of each month. You'll use these times to do your monthly planning. While monthly planning on top of quarterly planning may seem like a lot, I would highly recommend it.

Monthly planning serves two purposes: boosting motivation by marking accomplishments and keeping your plan on track by tweaking and adjusting for anything that got derailed, was finished ahead of schedule, or couldn't be finished as planned. If you work in a fast-paced environment, monthly plans may be even more relevant than quarterly plans.

In your monthly planning, start by reviewing if you've achieved all milestones originally planned for the month, ticking those off, and congratulating your team and yourself for those accomplishments.

Then look at any delays from your original plans. Brainstorm why those delays happened and ask if you could've have done anything differently. Give yourself ten to fifteen minutes, but not more, to dwell on this.

Now start looking forward again. What needs to be adjusted in the next month due to delays in the previous one?

Reflect on changes in priorities or new tasks or goals that have come up and factor these into your new planning. Decide on the utmost priorities for the upcoming months, based on accomplishments and delays. Create a modified copy of your quarterly plan based on this. You can keep your original quarterly plan so you can compare it to the modified versions at the end of the quarter or the year and figure out what lessons you've learned.

Next, take five to ten minutes and write down any challenges you're experiencing in your position. Are you feeling burned out? Are there tensions between people on your team? Have you had any issues with clients or beneficiaries? Are you dealing with too much pressure from your boss or the board? Write down all the challenges you're facing right now.

Take another five to ten minutes to brainstorm solutions to your challenges. What would you tell a friend or colleague if he or she came to you to share these challenges? This third-person perspective can be very helpful as it can provide you with some distance.

Write your answers down next to each challenge. Make a note on any point that you would like to discuss with your team or brainstorm with them on how to improve or solve a challenge. Add to the calendar any meetings needed to face these challenges.

By the end of your two hours of monthly planning you'll feel clear about goals and milestones achieved and empowered about the challenges and delays you and your team have been experiencing. You'll have a clear action plan to get back on track for the upcoming month and a list of points that need to be discussed with your team and other stakeholders.

Make sure to clearly communicate to your team the accomplishments of the months, things that weren't accomplished or were delayed. They should know the course corrections, the new goals, and the top priorities for the upcoming month.

* * *

In this chapter, we have reviewed organizational strategies that will help you, as a leader, have a clear vision of where you're going and where you're leading your team, and equally as important, how to get there.

The use of SMART goals, together with yearly, quarterly, and monthly planning, will allow you to, at any point in time, indicate to your team what the next steps are and whether you're on time or delayed. You can also celebrate with your team any milestones achieved.

You first need to get rid of that overwhelming feeling. As a leader, it's important to keep your focus and feeling overwhelmed is detrimental to focus. Don't try to implement everything at once, or you might start feeling overwhelmed again.

When you first start out planning like this, schedule only one activity you'd like to try out. For example, you could start by choosing two of your goals for the year and making them SMART. Or lay out your dates for yearly, quarterly, and monthly planning over the year. Make sure whatever you start with can be accomplished in thirty minutes to an hour. This time limit means you're more likely to get it done, and once you do, you'll feel a sense of accomplishment and possibility.

In the next chapter, we'll look into time-management strategies that will allow you to maintain a sense of control over your time and keep up-to-date with your planning and implementation.

CHAPTER 6
YOUR TIME-MANAGEMENT STRATEGIES

As she was driving to the office in the morning, Kai fielded four short calls from her assistant and a contractor. By the time she had sat down at her desk, she had already talked briefly with several team members and her assistant again. She worked for half an hour before Masao knocked on the door to talk about the upcoming board meeting for five minutes. When he left, two beneficiaries were already queuing to talk to her, while at the same time her boss called and five more emails came in.

If that sounds like your morning too, you're not alone. Landmark studies conducted by Henry Mintzberg in the seventies have shown that a manager's activities are "characterized by brevity, variety, and discontinuity."[29] In one study with chief executives, half of the activities they engaged in lasted less than nine minutes, and only 10% exceeded one hour.[30] In a more recent study of managers, project leaders and others, Dr. Gloria Mark from the University of California at Irving found that people spent, on average, only three minutes in any single event before being interrupted (or switching activities).[31]

When you become a team leader, the number of interruptions you get will usually be much higher than what you got as a team member. You'll have innumerable requests from your team members, your boss and colleagues. You'll field questions, complaints, conflicts, and requests for advice.

MANAGE INTERRUPTIONS

Maybe, in your new role as team leader, you're feeling a bit resistant and resentful of all these external requests on your time. You may feel it cuts into your productivity and interrupts your creative processes.

To deal with this, it's important you recognize that interruptions *will* happen and will now be a constant. Thus it's better to plan for them than to ignore them or hope that they'll go away. Recognize also that while being available to your team and other stakeholders is key and is part of your role as a team leader, you can gain some control over interruptions to protect your own productivity.

Compartmentalize

Create a time every day where all "management" activities take place. You can box in two or three management periods per day. For example, one before noon and one as your next-to-last item in the day.

This scheduling allows you to gain a measure of control over your day, as management duties can eat up your entire schedule if you let them. Make sure you clearly communicate your availability times to your team and other stakeholders and ask them to respect your "closed door" times. On your side, make sure to honour your commitment to being available at "open door" times and welcome anyone who comes knocking at the door, calling, or emailing.

My most productive and creative time is usually early in the morning. I like to schedule my first management time-box right after this time. If I get to work earlier than my team, by the time my team arrives and problems start arising, I've already completed at least two hours of focused creative work. I'm ready for a break and some human interaction.

Other people prefer to reserve the whole morning for creative work and compartmentalize their management time in the afternoon, or on the contrary, spend their mornings interacting with people and reserve the afternoon for creative, quiet work. In any case, it is good to test a few different options and see which is the best solution for your organizational situation and your personality.

Use this management time to talk to your team members, clients or beneficiaries, and colleagues. You can also answer requests and problem solve. This is the time where you wander about the office talking to people, pop into your colleague's department for a quick chat, make some calls, go check on progress with your team members, have a little informal chat with your boss and help your administrative assistant with any questions he might have. If the majority of your communication and requests happen by email, then you can use a big chunk of this management time to answer emails as well.

While you may have some specific activities scheduled to solve for this time, make sure there is ample room for things that just pop up.

Give people time to sort it out by themselves

You're the new leader, and you want to prove to your team what an amazing problem-solver you are. So you start every day by opening your emails and dutifully answering all requests. You stop whatever you are doing when one of your team members asks for help. You answer all calls on the spot. You interrupt your work to cross the campus to talk to someone in another department who wanted your help.

By the end of the week, you are far behind your plans and you are working evenings and weekends, feeling burned out and resentful. If this sounds like you, here's a little experiment you may wish to try out for a week.

Don't problem-solve *anything* before noon, either by email, telephone, or in person. If someone asks directly, tell them to try to solve them by themselves and, if it is not solved by noon, you'll help in the afternoon. You may be surprised to discover how many problems seem to get fixed without your input just by giving your team time to sort it out!

This experiment allows you to realize that it is OK to reserve quiet, creative times for your own work, as problems will still get solved in most cases, even if you are not immediately available. Allowing your team some time to figure things out by themselves has the added benefit of growing your team, as they'll become more creative at problem-solving if you are not as available to find a solution for them.

Limit your email time

Email is another one of those activities that can bleed into your whole day. You can use three techniques to deal with this.

First, compartmentalize email time. For example, you can make sure that inside your management time you leave one hour for emails. The majority of your email management will involve answering other people's requests as well, so it fits into this compartment. You can also set apart two email compartments per day, right after your management time-compartment, for instance.

Second, make sure you have a clear system for dealing with emails. Establish beforehand the possible actions for each email. Betsy and Warren Talbot, authors and creators of the podcast "An Uncluttered Life" suggests these four rules: every incoming email gets either: a) read and answered immediately; b) read and marked to solve later, in which case you schedule time for this in your calendar; c) immediately deleted or d) immediately archived if no response is required on your part.[32]

You can also create rules in your email software so that emails from different people arrive at different inboxes or files. You can then create special times to read each of those files.

Third, ask your team to write "searchable subject lines" for emails, that is email titles with keywords that allow you to easily search for that email later on, so you don't spend precious time looking up an archived email. Emails titled "Problem" or "Workshop" are not as search friendly as something titled "Urgent: venue for workshop XYZ not available on date requested."

There are a lot of good tips for managing email on the internet. If you're having trouble containing your email, make sure to read up on these tips and brainstorm possible solutions to get it under control.

MOVE FROM URGENT TO IMPORTANT

Time management experts recommend a useful diagram that helps understand how we use our time. It's called the urgent/important matrix and is often attributed to D. Eisenhower.[33]

Urgent activities require immediate attention and are usually linked to someone else's goals, not your own. We tend to focus on these because they have immediate consequences if we don't deal with them.

Important activities help you further your goals. They would normally be in your yearly and quarterly plans. They tend to have more long-term results and gains.

If you want to brainstorm which of your activities fit into each square, you can use the matrix provided in Clinic 10 of the Workbook.

The urgent versus important matrix.

	URGENT	NOT URGENT
IMPORTANT	1	2
NOT IMPORTANT	3	4

Square 1. Urgent and important. If you divide your activities into the four squares of the matrix, on Square 1 you would have things such as "completing end of year report by tomorrow," "solving bottle-neck in customer-service that's causing complaints," "answering the board's urgent request for a proposal." Square 1 will tend to absorb a lot of your mental energy. It contains unforeseeable crises, deadline-driven projects, last minute demands and a lot of things that got postponed from Square 2.

Square 2. Not urgent, important. Here you would find things such as "strategizing how to better reach ideal customers," "creating next year's content for programmes," "researching the new trends and evidence in my knowledge area." It contains activities related to longer-term returns, such as strategizing, working towards goals, and relationship building, for which we rarely have any feeling of urgency.

Square 3. Urgent, not important. It contains most of your phone calls, emails, and interruptions. It may also contain some reports required by others, which are not important to you or your team. Or it could contain some meetings which you're required to attend last minute, and in general, other people's unimportant but time-constrained requests. Activities in this quadrant can be deceitful because they make you feel busy and useful since you're putting out fires. But putting out those fires does not further your main goals.

Square 4. Not urgent, not important. Here you'll find time-wasting activities like browsing social media, reading the news (unless you are a journalist), filing and archiving, unconstrained and goal-less web-browsing (as opposed to goal-focused research on the web), and all of the activities you normally engage in when procrastinating. These activities act like a strong magnet, and we're easy prey to them, especially when we're tired, hungry, or unclear about our way forward, as they're a way of avoiding decisions and not thinking. However, they leave us with a distinct taste of futility and restlessness.

Square 2, important but not urgent activities, is clearly the place where you want to spend most of your time, as it will help you advance your longer term goals and represents true productivity. Unfortunately, because of lack of urgency, these activities tend to get relegated to the back of the line, even though they could bring great results or revenue in the medium to long term. Mostly, they don't have a deadline, which makes them even harder to prioritize.

Many times you'll find that you're "trapped" on Square 1 activities, with a double sense of urgency and importance. Spending a lot of time on Square 1 can lead to burnout, as it feels like you're putting out fires all the time with no chance to breathe and refocus.

Thus, your goal is to try to move away from Square 1 activities towards Square 2 ones. One way to ensure Square 2 activities get done, despite the lack of a deadline, is to make sure you reserve some time every week (at least 4-6 hours) to focus *exclusively* on non-urgent but highly important activities. Make sure you alot high-quality hours to this strategic time-compartment. Make it a sacred space.

You may be thinking you can never justify dedicating four to six hours of quality time to non-urgent but important activities when you have three deadlines coming up.

Let's try and turn this reasoning around. Because those other three activities have deadlines, you're ensuring they'll get done no matter what. You've never missed a deadline before and you aren't going to start now. So even if you have to pull an all-nighter, you know you are going to make those deadlines.

The non-deadline-based important activities, on the other hand, are the ones at risk of getting put off week after week if you don't reserve some quality time to tackle them. Also, the more you make time for solid planning and strategizing, the fewer fires you'll have to deal with, and the more the burden of activities in Square 1 will decrease.

As for Squares 3 and 4 activities, your goal is to minimize them. Start by tackling Square 3. These activities are tricky because, due to their urgency, they might actually feel important. Think hard about the activities that feel urgent and ask whether they're really furthering your goals. They might be other people's priorities, not your own.

We've already covered some approaches to be less reactive to other people's requests and protect your quality time, such as compartmentalization and waiting before you intervene, which you can use to decrease Square 3 activities from eating up your time.

Another tool is delegation, which we'll cover below. By delegating email handling or phone calls to an assistant, for example, you avoid falling prey to reactive behaviour, and you can choose when to return those phone calls or emails.

The strongest tool to combat activities in Square 4--and many in Square 3--is awareness of how much of your time they eat up. You raise your awareness in several ways. The first one is tracking your time-use. Laura Vanderkam, a time-management expert, who covers this issue extensively in her books and blogs, uses a simple spreadsheet called "168-hours[34]" that you can use to track every single fifteen-minute span of your week's activities. You can of course, also create your own spreadsheet to your taste. Alternatively, you can use a time-management app. There are a lot out there, and many of them are free. I share some of my favourites in the Notes and References section.[35]

Doing this time-tracking exercise, even if only for a week, can be extremely powerful. You'll be shocked to realize how much time we actually "waste" in non-productive activities, such as web-browsing, social media, watching TV or videos, filing and archiving or whatever your preferred procrastination activity is. Even if you "only" spend around thirty minutes per day on these activities, by adding them up over a five-day work week, you'll end up with two and a half hours. Enough time to write a blog post, or have three meetings, or even leave more time for personal activities, such as exercising or home-cooking.

A second way to raise your awareness consists of setting an alarm to ring five times a day at random times. Every time it sounds, ask yourself: is this activity truly important? Is it furthering my goals? You can track how many times a day these alarms catch you in non-important activities.

Finally, recognize that we fall into Square 3 and Square 4 activities because staying in Square 2 (or even Square 1) takes a lot of willpower. And willpower is a finite resource that dwindles over the day as we use it up.[36] Thus many times we might not have as much willpower in the afternoon or evening as we do in the morning. A good strategy is, therefore, to schedule your Square 2 activities at earlier times when you're not only at your most creative, but also when you still have a good stock of willpower so you will actually get these activities done.

A short break or a nap after a period of work can partially refill your willpower stocks during the day. If at all possible in your organizational setting, do something that brings you pleasure, rest, and a deeper satisfaction than mindless web-browsing. For example, you could use your lunch time to go for a walk, read a book, take a short nap or exercise.

DELEGATE

My sister is an architect with a thriving business. Some years ago, however, things were not going so well. She was feeling overwhelmed and burned out. Delving into it, she found that one thing in particular was compounding on the situation: her assistant.

Her assistant was very social and helped keep the office in good cheer. But she did a poor job at most of the tasks my sister assigned her, was not proactive in any way, nor interested in learning, and didn't pay attention to details. One time she managed to write out three wrong checks in a row.

Still, my sister wouldn't let go of her. Her arguments were varied: the lady was honest and she could trust her with money. She kept up a good ambiance in the office. My sister didn't have time to go through the hiring process. It was her own responsibility for not training her enough. With what she was willing to pay, she couldn't get someone better. Plus, a feeling of "what if whoever comes next is worse?"

Finally, the assistant made one too many grave mistakes. My sister fired her and hired a man named Oscar to fill the spot. When I asked her how it was going, she told me this story: a few days ago she had asked Oscar to send a package to a particular client. Used as she was to her previous assistant, she told him she would send him the instructions on how to proceed, which delivery service to use, and the client's address in a text message later on. An hour later, before she had time to even start sending him the instructions, the client called her to acknowledge receipt of the package. Oscar had taken it into his own hands to solve the problem, had looked up the address of the client in the files, found out the quickest way to deliver the package, and proceeded.

In the span of some weeks, Oscar managed to turn the office around and my sister's working life with it. Finally, she could delegate confidently and focus on the most important things for her business.

Delegating effectively is on you as a leader. If a member of your team is not doing a good job despite consistent training, it is time to let go and find someone new. If, on the other hand, you have people to whom you can delegate effectively and you're not doing it, then you are doing a disservice to yourself *and* to your team. Trust is one of the most important things you can give your team members. Many times, when we are not delegating, it boils down to lack of trust in others to do things properly.

Common reasons why we'd rather not delegate include:

- "These things are all my responsibility; I can't really delegate any of them."
- "I'm not even sure what I could delegate."
- "It'll take me longer to teach the other person how to do this properly than do it myself."
- "I will still need to check it, edit it, or supervise it, so it is easier to just do it myself from the start."
- "No one can do this as perfectly as I can."
- "I can't trust anyone with this; it's too important or sensitive."
- "My team will realize that my tasks are not that complicated or difficult and they can do them too, so there's no reason for me to be the team leader."

- "It took me a long time to learn this; why would I just give out my secret to someone else so that they can do it?"

These "reasons" not to delegate can be grouped into several main categories: a lack of awareness of what activities we could actually delegate and to whom, a perception of lack of time, of lack of skills in others, or of lack of confidence in ourselves.

Lack of awareness of delegable activities.

When you're just familiarizing yourself with a new role, you might find it hard to figure out what activities you can take on and which you can ask others to do.

Going back to some of the exercises in this book on goal-setting may help with this. Bring together two documents and pore over them for a while: your quarterly and monthly planning and the report of your time-management app or the spreadsheet where you recorded all your activities for at least a week or two. Look at all these activities and categorize them into four categories:

a. Those you excel at doing and which you love to do.
b. Those you're really good at but you're not really passionate about.
c. Those you can do, if you have to, but you neither like doing them nor are exceptionally good at it.
d. Things you are not good at doing and which you despise.

Activities in columns c and d do not fall into your key areas of competence. Because you're not good at them and you resist doing them, they'll normally eat up more time than needed. These are prime suspects for delegation. With the profile of your team members at hand, determine if it would be of more value to delegate these to someone else. In Clinic 11 in the Workbook, you will find a table where you can carry out this exercise in delegating.

If the list of activities is long and includes mostly administrative tasks, you might consider, if you don't have one yet, hiring an administrative assistant (or a virtual assistant). Another option, if financial or accounting issues are what eats up most of your time or are what you are worst at, is hiring an accountant or a bookkeeper. If you spend a lot of time editing other people's work, you might benefit from hiring an editor part-time. If social media is your headache, delegate to a social media expert.

If you work for a company or organization, a clear list of activities and the time they consume can be an important tool in negotiating with your boss or HR for hiring someone new or receiving support from finance or admin assistants or the communication department inside the company.

While working as a team leader at a hospital, I wasted a lot of hours working through the hospital bureaucracy. I hated this. It drove me crazy to have to call on people again and again to ask if a process was moving forward, only to hear some piece of paper was still missing.

Then a research assistant offered to take some of these activities into her own hands. I still had to coach her on the paperwork processes and who to contact, but my level of frustration went down immediately and I gained more hours to dedicate to other work. Also, I realized that she *loved* doing this type of work! Incomprehensibly to me, she found pursuing people and figuring out the bureaucracy maze a challenging and rewarding task.

So if you are finding it unfair to delegate tasks you dislike, think that your headache might be someone else's bliss. Someone always likes to do the activities we despise. Look for that person, whether inside or outside your team. Letting your team members try some new tasks can boost their confidence, and you might discover a hidden gem.

Lack of time.

You recognize delegating might be a good option, but you're so overwhelmed that you feel like it's faster to do it yourself. This, however, lands you straight back on Square 1 or Square 3 of the urgent versus important landscape. It doesn't help you to move towards Square 2.

Can you imagine yourself saying, "I don't buy property because it is a waste of money?" Probably not, right? Buying property does indeed require laying down a big amount of money, but it's rarely seen as a money-waster. It's an investment.

Training your people so you can delegate to them is also an investment. It costs time now, but you'll reap the benefits later in the same currency: more time. In this case, more time for you to focus on strategic activities that land you straight in Square 2.

In much the same way as you compartmentalize time for Square 2 activities every week, make sure you compartmentalize time to grow and train your team members in activities that are now consuming your time and that you could easily delegate.

The same goes for the time-investment required for hiring a new person. If you're overwhelmed, it's a smart investment of your very limited time. Still, be sure to brainstorm how to delegate parts of this process to someone else. Maybe your HR department can take care of all the first screenings, maybe one of your team members is a whizz at interviewing.

You'll still need to spend time on this, deciding on the exact job profile you or your team needs, and performing at least the final interviews. But the right choice of person will make you reap the time benefits of your investment.

Lack of skills in others.

If you should be delegating certain tasks to, say, Chris, but you're not doing it because he lacks skills, consider your options: you can of course just do his job for him, taking on too many responsibilities, but keeping yourself stuck in Square 1.

You can train him (or send him to training) in those skills. With enough training and motivation, in most cases Chris will be able to do what you need from him. Make sure you're willing and able to spend time consistently training this person.

Don't expect perfect performance from the beginning. While you may think he's not doing this task as perfectly as you can, ask yourself how important it is that things get done perfectly, compared to the time you're gaining.

You might still need to do corrections or supervise work occasionally, but in most cases this will require less time from you than preparing something from scratch. Also, if you are providing feedback, chances are next time Chris will produce an even better version, which will require less input from you.

In some cases, you will find out that no matter how much training you give, Chris is still not performing up to what you need. While it is worth taking time to reflect whether this is a communication problem on your side, too high expectations, or a need for more training, it's also worth considering whether Chris is just not the adequate fit for this activity or for your team. Everybody is able to learn new skills, but not everybody is willing.

Lastly, if Chris really is just not performing up to what you need, it might be time to let him go and bring in someone new. Letting go of someone is a difficult decision. As we saw from my sister's example, it is easy to find reasons why not to do it.

Christine Kane, founder and CEO of Uplevel You, shares a great test for whether it's time to let go of someone: consider how much of your mental space he or she occupies.[37]

You're not normally preoccupied with your best team members or their work. You just think of them when working with them, when praising them, or when giving them a hand with something. When someone is not performing well, though, as was the case with my sister's assistant, that team member takes up a lot of your mental space, between worrying, solving mistakes, and completing tasks that this person didn't do. If one team member is occupying too much mental space, this is a powerful sign that it might be time to let go and bring in someone new.

Lack of confidence in ourselves.

Are you failing to delegate because you feel like people will figure out anyone can do these tasks? Are you afraid that, if you share how to do these tasks, someone might steal your job?

Hoarding tasks and information so that everyone "needs" you means you're basing your leadership on the wrong traits. You've been made a team leader because someone saw you were leadership material. Not because of particular tasks you're good at. A great leader is a great delegator.

If you haven't already done so, go back to the first chapter of the book and figure out the skills that make you a great leader. If you have listed your skills, go look back at your list. Those skills are surely more than being "great at calling customers" or "a fantastic report writer."

You bring people together. You're proactive. You take responsibility. You think outside of the box. You inspire people. You're great at organizing, synergizing, and delivering. This is what makes you a leader.

Recognize the true reasons and fears that hold you back from delegating. Then recognize that delegating will *enhance* your leadership. It will give you more time for true leadership tasks, for growing your team, strategizing, and moving things forward. Delegating will show your team you trust them, and people are attracted to leaders who make them grander. Be the one who grows your team.

Delegating effectively

Once you've faced the reasons you don't delegate, you may want to put together a strategy for delegating effectively. Start with the list of delegable tasks you drew up earlier in the chapter. Choose one task and brainstorm the right person to delegate it to.

Stephen Covey categorizes delegation into gofer (someone you just send to "go for" something) and stewardship delegation,[38] which I like to call methods-oriented and results-oriented delegation.

In methods-oriented delegation, you focus on the how. You tell people exactly how to do the task and micromanage the details of it. If you've ever been on the receiving end of this type of delegation, you know it's not very motivating and creates a lot of resentment. Most of us don't like being micromanaged.

In results-based delegation, you focus on the end product, and you trust the person to come up with the how. This trust improves creativity and fosters responsibility. To make sure this system works, you need several components:

a. A clear mutual understanding of **what the end result will look like**. If you can work with the person to ensure this end result comes out of inputs from both of you, you'll have a lot more of a buy-in, as the person will feel more ownership for the project.

b. Make sure to explain the **importance of the end result** for you, the organization, or the beneficiaries, as well as the **benefits** for the person accomplishing the task (learning, new skills, improved performance, bonuses, vacations, recognition, etc.)

c. A **deadline** for when the result needs to be ready. I strive to explain to my team members *why* we need the result by that deadline so they won't feel it's a whim on my side.

d. **Any major restrictions**. You don't want to give too specific guidelines so as not to fall into micromanagement. But you should ensure the person knows which methods are acceptable and not acceptable inside your organization, or for this particular task.

e. Valuable information about **what has worked and not worked before**. Don't ask people to reinvent the wheel and don't deprive them of potential lessons learned from your mistakes or those of others.

f. **Check-in times and milestones**. Let the person propose to you when she or he wants to meet between now and the deadline to discuss progress and brainstorm obstacles. Agree on what this progress will look like (use SMART goals). Once you have an agreement, put it in writing. I normally recommend at least weekly check-ins, even if short ones, as they help to keep people motivated.

g. The **resources they can count on**, including support and training from you, and the mechanisms to ask for this support. Make sure they know how to make you keep your promise of support and that they feel confident in asking for it.

Once all of this is clear and agreed upon, let go. Trust the person to do the right work, and make sure to keep your end of the deal. Maintain motivation and accountability by showing up for the agreed check-in times and helping to problem-solve any obstacles.

* * *

In this chapter, we've reviewed time-management strategies that will, together with your organizational and planning strategies, help you stay on top of all your new responsibilities as a leader.

To be effective as a leader, you'll need to set up strategies to deal with the numerous interruptions and requests on your time. It'll also be key for you to identify which tasks will truly move you forward, which are only reactive and responding to other people's needs, and which are a waste of time. Make sure to have an Urgent versus Important Square clearly visible in your office, and add your tasks, on sticky notes or on the whiteboard, to each square.

Plan your day to support your Square 2 activities as much as possible. The strategies that will help you do this include compartmentalizing, limiting your email time, giving other people time to sort things out by themselves, and delegating effectively.

As we discussed before, don't try to implement everything at once, or you risk starting to feel overwhelmed again. Start by trying out one new time-management technique that you want to implement for a week or two and add up from there. For example, create weekly time-compartments, which are exclusively for Square 2 activities. Or start by making a list of tasks you can delegate.

One last comment: when you try out tips we've covered in this chapter or the previous one that seem to work for you, share them. Spend some time coaching one or two people in your team on them. Grow your team. Everybody benefits, including you.

This brings us to the end of Part II, where we concerned ourselves with the mindsets and strategies needed to grow yourself as a leader. In Part III we'll discuss how to lead a team. We'll start by understanding how teams are formed, how we can positively influence that process, and what characteristics successful teams have. Then we'll move on to the major maker or breaker of teams--communication.

PART III

LEADING YOUR TEAM

Chapter 7

Team formation

Imagine you're part of a successful team that's been working together for a while. You celebrate birthdays, go for Friday happy-hour, and know the names of everyone's kids and partners and pets. One day, your team leader quits and a new person comes in. This person starts with a meeting in which he or she explains the new working strategy, new goals, and new work allocations.

The division of tasks, however, doesn't really reflect each of your strengths and passions. Also, the sacred Wednesday afternoon meeting has been changed to Friday, which used to be the day you all left work a bit earlier to go for happy-hour together. To top it off, when your colleague Carol, whom you all call Cal, asks a question, the new leader answers: "Yes, Carrie, thank you for bringing that up."

How would such a scenario make you feel? This may just be a made-up example, but similar situations happen every day in many working environments. New leaders come in and don't take time to get to know their teams. In their eagerness to implement their new ideas, they forget to acknowledge and show respect for previous traditions and methods.

Taking time to know your team, whether it's an established

team or you're putting together a new one, is key to ensuring your best chance for success. While it may seem like a waste of time, it'll pay off later with a stronger team and will help you avoid a lot of headaches in the future.

Now that you've spent some time solidifying your skills and strategies for managing yourself as a leader, you're ready to start building and growing your team. First, by getting to know them as individuals and sowing the seeds to constructive relationships with each of them. Then by understanding and managing the team formation process your team, whether just put together or already established, will go through.

GETTING TO KNOW YOUR TEAM MEMBERS

Getting to know your team members is crucial for several reasons. First, it shows you care. And we've already talked about how important caring is. Second, it makes people feel listened to. We all love to talk about ourselves, but most of us don't get many opportunities to do so. Imagine how cool it would be if your current boss or team leader calls you in for a one-hour personal interview because she wants to get to know you better. Third, it gives you a better idea of areas where your team members will need coaching and how to best motivate them. Finally, it gives your team members a clearer idea of who you are and what you stand for, partially by showing and partially by telling.

To get to know your team members, you can plan initial one-on-one interviews with each of them. Clinic 12 in the Workbook contains a template you may want to use for these interviews.

While you'll be doing most of the listening, you can still use this opportunity to explain why you believe you need to get to know each of them. You can explain your vision, your team values, your decision-making process, and possibly even how you evaluate performance.

In Chapter 2, you had some time to reflect on your team composition, while in Chapter 4, you had an opportunity to map out the things you know and ignore about each of your team members, both from a personal and a professional standpoint. Here you'll start filling in the gaps around all the things you don't know about them.

So, what should this interview be about? Mainly, try to remember that this interview is *about your team member*, not about you. You'll be listening for about 75-80% of the time and do no more than 20-25% of the talking.

Plan your interviews in advance, and make sure you book enough time for each of them. Then send your team members individual emails asking them to meet with you. Briefly explain the general purpose of the meeting as perhaps "getting to know each other," "getting acquainted," or something similar. Explaining what the meeting is about helps relieve any anxiety people might be feeling over, for instance, the possibility of being fired.

Explain the purpose and agenda. Start the meeting by thanking the person for being here. Then re-explain the purpose of the meeting, this time in more detail. Briefly describe the structure you'd like to follow, so they know what to expect. Let them know you'd first like to know more about them, their skills, experiences, and values. Then you'd like to move on to talking about the company, the project, and the team, getting their views on things that are working well plus any ideas they have for improvements or new projects. Finally, you'd like to discuss what hasn't been working well or could be improved. Also, let them know they'll have time at the end of the interview to ask any questions they have about you and your vision for the team.

If you like to write things down for later, make sure you let them know, from the beginning, that you'll be taking notes. As the interview unfolds, write brief notes and look back at the person, as maintaining eye-contact is important for people to feel listened to.

Background and experience. Start people off easy by asking about their background and past experience, both in previous companies and in the current one. This helps you establish a rapport and makes the other person more comfortable. Don't interrupt. If you want to ask a question, write it down and ask it when your team member has finished answering the current one.

What works. Move on to more insightful questions but remain on the positive side of things for now. Ask them to describe their position and responsibilities. What part of their current tasks and responsibilities do they enjoy the most? What skills do they love to use? What projects have they worked on that have been the most rewarding and why? Which accomplishments are they proudest of?

What could be improved. Switch to discussing areas of challenges and opportunity. If you've done your listening well, the person will now, hopefully, trust you enough to share some of the things he or she thinks aren't going so well. Ask about the skills they're not using and would love to use, ask if they feel as if any part of their skill-set is being underused or underestimated.

What parts of their current job or responsibilities don't they like, and why? What do they consider to be the team's most pressing challenges or areas for improvement? What organizational issues do they think aren't working well?

As you close out this last part, ask them if they have anything else they'd like to add, anything that's on their minds. This open-ended question can sometimes bring great returns, so it's worth asking.

Close the meeting. Lastly, ask them if they have any questions for you. Answer them honestly, or, if you can't, explain the reason why you can't answer it (e.g., confidential, you'd rather discuss it with everyone present in a team meeting, you need time to reflect on it, or whatever). If you don't know something, don't make up an answer. Say you don't know the answer and you'll do your best to find out.

Close the meeting by thanking your team member again and letting him or her know these sort of meetings will start happening on a regular basis.

When your team member leaves, spend five minutes reviewing the meeting. Check your notes, and add anything still on your mind. Include any ideas for how this person's skills could be put to better use, areas of opportunity for training and growth, and any other notes. Schedule time to follow up on any commitments you made during the meeting, and set a date to get back to your team member with the information. Keeping your commitment will strengthen the trust you're building with your team members.

Repeat this exercise with each person on your team. By the end of it, you'll have a much clearer understanding of each of them, the team as a whole, and your challenges and opportunities.

After you've hired a new team member, make sure you go through this process with this new person as well, especially if you didn't conduct the hiring interviews.

FROM INDIVIDUALS TO A TEAM

At the beginning of the book, I shared an anecdote about going to a leadership camp in the forest in my early twenties. I will use this example here again to illustrate how teams get formed so let's review the story briefly. I was put in a group with nine complete strangers, and we had six hours to complete a series of challenges in the woods. These challenges required teamwork and included things like walking on suspended cables, balancing a huge see-saw, and getting everybody up and over a fence.

Not only was this one-day exercise a lot of fun, but also it gave us a one-day condensed version of the path all teams go through when they get formed.

When you have a collection of individuals, you might call it a group, and yet *a group is not necessarily the same as a team*[39]. In a group, each individual has his or her own interests and agenda. A team emerges when the members have a common sense of purpose. This doesn't mean individual agendas will disappear (and you need to be aware of individual agendas, as we'll discuss below), but that common cause will take precedence over individual agendas.

However, a true team doesn't just automatically emerge when you put your team members in a room and give them a common cause. Research dating back to the 1960s by Bruce Tuckman has shown that disparate teams go through similar steps in their formation.[40] These stages are usually called *forming, storming, norming,* and *performing*. While other researchers have come up with modifications, these steps have endured the test of time. They provide a good framework for understanding the team development process. Just as any other development process (e.g., a child learning to walk), the team formation process is not always linear and can have setbacks.

Most of us have at some point lived through these steps without being aware of them. As we discuss them, think back to any time you joined a team or a committee (e.g., the parent's committee at your kid's school, a basketball team, a group of experts coming together for a one-day evaluation exercise, a college study team) and see whether you can identify the different stages.

The **forming stage** is the "testing the waters" stage. People remain polite and on their best behaviour. Team members are "sizing each other up" and figuring out how they fit into the team. There can be excitement, anticipation, and optimism, but also anxiety. (How am I going to fit in? Am I the dumbest in the group? Do these people have what it takes for us to succeed?) The task ahead and the responsibilities for each person are still unclear, but people start feeling part of a bigger something--a team.

Think back to any time where you joined a group or team, for example for a project in college. This is the phase at the initial meeting where you try to gauge who will want to take control of the task, who's the free-rider, who's the perfectionist, etc., while also trying to appear cooperative.

In my leadership camp experience, this stage happened in the first minutes before we actually got down to tackling the first task. People were smiling, cheering and highly motivated. Also, we were all secretly gauging who were the fastest and strongest in the group, and who the weakest links.

The **storming stage** is the "there's-no-way-we're-doing-it-like-that" stage. Here, politeness and best behaviour tend to break down and personal agendas and preferences emerge, along with intragroup conflict. Conflict arises from the misalignment between individual agendas and each of these agendas with the team's agenda. Agendas may have to do with what the outcome should look like or with individual preferences on how to achieve it.

If you've been in an evaluation committee, you may have haggled over how to proceed with the evaluation and what the characteristics of the best project or candidate are. If you've been part of a PTA group organizing the school's end-of-year festivities, you may have argued over whether you wanted a party in the gym, a fair, or a sports and academic competition.

Conflict will also arise over who leads the group. Even if a leader was clearly set up from the beginning, his or her leadership may be challenged. Team members may vie for attention and try to establish themselves in a particular position, resulting in subtle or not so subtle power struggles.

On the task side of things, people get frustrated and dissatisfied because things aren't advancing and are hampered by conflict. People can also feel overwhelmed if the task seems huge and the way forward unclear, or if they feel uncomfortable with the approach being proposed. At this stage, in reaction to all of the above, people may even question the task assigned to the team and how worthwhile it is.

This stage arrived for my team in the woods as soon as we tackled the first task: balancing a giant see-saw. People started vying for power, trying to impose their own views on how to accomplish the task and speaking over each other. We quickly got frustrated when we realized that we had no clue as to how to get over this seemingly simple obstacle.

Most of us hate this stage; yet, it's a natural stage of team formation, and it can be handled so that it goes by as quickly and painlessly as possible. When you are struggling through it, keep in mind that it's a normal stage and you and your team will get past it.

The **norming stage** is the "this-is-how-we-do-it" stage. On the human side of the equation, the team members reach a consensus on acceptable group behaviour, and each person's role inside the team is established. The team agrees or gains clarity on how the task is to be accomplished and on roles and responsibilities. With this comes a renewed feeling of empowerment and motivation. The big decisions are made by group consensus and the small ones delegated to particular individuals. Commitment to the shared goal strengthens along with unity. Individuals also accept or resign themselves to aspects they don't particularly like, which are relegated in favour of the common goal.

At my leadership camp, we reached this stage by the end of the first task, when we finally managed to balance the see-saw. The second task in the woods became easier as we reached a tacit consensus on who was in charge, and that complaining and bickering were not allowed. We became better at listening to each other, speaking in turns, and encouraging each other forward.

The **performing stage** is the "we're-doing-it" stage. The team's structure at this point is fully functional and accepted by all. The focus and energy of the group is on the common task, not on vying for power or understanding the group. The team is cohesive and self-supporting. Team members look after each other and help each other out.

At this point the team requires less intervention and support from you. Your job has more to do with delegating tasks and providing particular assistance or coaching. You clear the way through issues that lie outside the team, provide support with personal and interpersonal development, and bring all the different components together towards the end goal. At the performing stage, results start to emerge.

After the first two tasks, our team in the woods started breezing past the remaining ones. We even had time at lunch to fool around and make human pyramids, just for laughs. We were moving forward, having fun together, and supporting all members of the team as we each faced our fears at the different tasks. Thanks to that remarkable support, I was even able to jump off from a cliff, to be carried away by a zip line.

Note, disagreement and conflict will still happen here, but in many cases they can be resolved without the need for leadership intervention. They'll rarely have to do with the types of conflict seen in the storming stage. Also, several factors, such as changes in tasks, members coming in or leaving, or outside organizational changes can lead the team to cycle back to an earlier stage.

The **termination/ending stage**. This stage wasn't part of Tuckman's original model but has been recognized as important in later years, as many teams do come to a natural end after their common goal is accomplished.

At this stage, members may experience strong feelings ranging from elation at the goal being accomplished to sadness at the impending separation from team members. Individual and team morale may fluctuate accordingly during the final stages. It is important for the team members and for you as a team leader to recognize that, in some respects, this stage resembles a grieving process and that managing it as such can sometimes help.

MANAGING THE TEAM FORMATION STAGES

While in most cases, teams will go through all these phases, the time that a particular team spends in the first three phases can vary greatly. This variation hints at aspects that can be improved to shorten these phases and facilitate the transition to the performing stage.

In the forest leadership camp experience I shared above, we basically went through the forming to the performing stage in a couple of hours or less. At the time, I knew nothing about these team development stages, but in retrospect, I can easily identify the turning point when we went from storming to norming. For us, that point came when we were trying to balance the giant see-saw. It had five seats per side and the whole team had to be split between the two sides of the see-saw so that it would reach equilibrium.

We had been at it for quite a long time, with everyone shouting instructions or moving from one side to the other in complete disarray. Then our facilitator kindly pointed out that we had used up a whole hour on a single task and had only five more hours to complete the eleven remaining ones!

We quickly stopped bickering. People started accepting particular roles. Two leaders emerged naturally and guided the group into finally balancing the see-saw in less than ten minutes.

Taking a lesson from this experience, one great way of managing the team formation stages is through time constraints: clear deadlines on when the first task should be accomplished can help propel the forming, storming, and norming phases.

You can combine time constraints with a pre-chosen physical setting that brings your whole team together. For example, you can book a conference room for a whole morning or plan a whole day--or even weekend--retreat. You then invite the whole team to this contained setting. You plan ice-breaking and introduction exercises, explain the common goal, and use participatory approaches to emerge at the end of the meeting with a clear roadmap with roles, responsibilities, and milestones. You then take a step back and act as a facilitator and an observer.

You can also use stage-specific strategies to manage the process. You can apply these in your retreat exercise or during your normal office work, in particular when you lay out a new task, put together a new sub-team, or new team members join.

Forming stage

A good orientation or kick-off process is useful in many settings. It basically consists of bringing your team together for a predefined period of time with three aims in mind. First, to help the team members get to know each other. Second, to help the team members understand and clarify the teams' mission and, potentially, how to accomplish the goals. Third, to grow trust and cooperation.

For the first aim, you can use ice-breakers to help your team get to know each other better. This is particularly important if individuals don't know each other at all but can even be useful when people have already been working together for a while.

For the second aim, you can start by sharing with your team the general, overarching goals, and then engaging them in a brainstorming session to discuss other goals, in line with the organizations' ones, which the team would like to add. You will find a format template, "Conducting Participatory Approaches," on how to run these brainstorming exercises in Clinic 13 of the accompanying Workbook.

After discussing goals, let the team brainstorm the how and the who. Basically, ask them the same questions you asked yourself when doing your yearly or quarterly planning. How do they think the tasks can be broken down into milestones? How long will each activity take? Who do they think is the best person to take up each activity? How do you make each goal a SMART one?

Because you've already done this exercise yourself, you'll be in a great position to guide the team through the big roadblocks you've already found. Plus, you'll have some ideas to share if the team gets stuck. However, this prior experience may also make it harder for you to keep an open mind to new ideas that emerge from the team. Particularly if they're very different from your carefully laid out plan. Agree with yourself beforehand that this exercise will add new richness and insight to your plan, so you can be welcoming and not judgmental of new ideas.

Finally, another exercise you can use to help your team go through the forming process is to create a team identity. This is a participatory exercise where your team comes up with a name for the team. (And even a slogan or a logo, if you want.)

To find a name, you can start by establishing the goals of the team, and then together brainstorm words they associate with the team's goals and personality. The best way is to find a team name by consensus, but if this doesn't work, voting can also be used. Clinic 14 "Creating a Team Identity" in the Workbook contains a step-by-step template that you can use as a basis to conduct this process.

Storming stage

When the storming stage starts, some of us feel like fleeing the room. It's discouraging to see people disagreeing over the set task or arguing over small details. They'll vie for attention and try to impose their own way of doing things. But remember that moving into the storming stage also means you're actually getting closer to the norming and performing stages!

Storming stages may happen not only when you bring together a new group of individuals who don't know each other, but also--less frequently or acutely--when you bring together your team to work on a new task. Individuals can storm over what the task should look like and how to get there, and especially when individuals don't know each other, over the roles that each individual assumes in the team.

In the storming stage, it's essential to acknowledge the conflict and speak openly about it. Your role is to lead this process and manage it in a positive way. Give people a defined amount of time to vent their disagreements and complaints. Carefully manage the framework in which these are vented, e.g., no insults, no criticizing the other person, only the ideas.

After this venting time is over, move the team on to problem-solving. You'll want them to focus on problem-solving both the group processes (e.g., agree on conflict management approaches) and the task-related issues (e.g., if the goal seems too complicated and unclear, break it down into smaller steps; redefine and rethink roles and milestones; brainstorm new approaches; and so on).

In Chapters 10 and 11, we will look into conflict management approaches that can be helpful through the storming stage.

Norming stage

At the norming stage, the team is finally finding common ground and reaching agreements. Make sure you facilitate the process as much as possible without interfering.

Help by taking assistant roles, such as writing down ideas, moderating whose turn it is to speak and moving people on to the next issue when the discussion gets repetitive. Be careful to keep the team within the constraints of the organization's mission, vision, and values, as well as the team's main goals, by providing them with reality-checks.

You can suggest exercises to help your team come up with some basic, general team agreements. The first one of these agreements is a team "manifesto" or team charter, a statement or a declaration of what the team stands for. Below you'll find one example. In the Workbook, Clinic 15 has an exercise template you and your team can use to create a team charter of your own. It also contains examples of other team or organizational manifestos you can use as inspiration.

Here's an example of one of my teams' charter:

- When in doubt, we ask what is best for the beneficiaries or end users.
- We ask questions first, give our own opinion second.
- We mirror what the other person is saying to make sure we understood.
- We base our arguments on evidence.
- We focus on problem-solving.
- We take care of one another.
- We celebrate other people's successes and our own.
- We strive to see every challenge as a growth opportunity.
- We have fun and take pleasure in our work.

The second agreement is the team's meeting rules. This

includes guidelines such as when and how meetings happen, who calls them, moderator and minute-taking roles, and so on. As most teams will have regular meetings, meetings will become the main space where the team will come together. Having some basic rules can make meetings more efficient and more constructive. Clinic 16 in the Workbook has some general meeting rules, which could be a starting point for discussing your team's own rules.

Performing stage

Now your team is working well together, but your leadership role isn't over. Even when things are moving, your role is still double. On the strategic side, maintain momentum by helping with participatory team evaluations, highlighting milestones and goals achieved. You can discuss challenges and brainstorm potential solutions. Ensure smooth flow by solving any outside obstacles the team may be facing and by serving as a link with other teams or departments, and also between the different individuals in your own team.

On the human side, your role to promote and maintain growth, motivation, a team spirit, and a good atmosphere is just as important. Celebrate milestones achieved and support your teams' ideas for friendly and appealing activities (birthday celebrations, off-work get together events, acknowledgement boards). You can facilitate continuing education through coaching, setting up external training, or initiating discussions with other players. Finally, you can help maintain on-going communication and step in when conflict arises (see Chapters 8 to 11).

Adjourning stage

When your team reaches the end of a task or goal, and especially if the team is to be dissolved afterwards, you'll find another stage when you as a leader might need to step up. You can smooth out the process by helping the team keep their focus on completing the last deliverables, despite the impending changes and managing the "grieving" process, if there is one.

On the strategic side, have a closing session with an evaluation of the teams' processes and accomplishments and lead the team in identifying lessons learned. This is an invaluable process for everyone--team members, you, the organization. Make sure a short summary of this evaluation is created and shared widely, inside and outside the team.

On the human side, create a closing celebration where contributions from all team members are acknowledged and individuals can speak up and share what they're taking with them from this experience, and what next steps they're planning. This get-together formally acknowledges the closure of this team and helps individuals cope with the impending changes by celebrating together and looking into the future.

THE NORMS OF SUCCESSFUL TEAMS

What makes a team great? Some years ago, Google decided to put its huge collective mind and analytical power to work in answering this question. They set up a team called "Project Aristotle" tasked with finding an answer by using Google's immense collection of data on its own employees and teams.[41]

The task wasn't easy. The teams rated as the best at Google were disparate. There were no trends suggesting combinations of individuals with certain personality types, skills, or backgrounds made for better teams. Some great teams were composed of people that socialized and were friends outside of the office, while others were not. Some groups had strong team leaders, while in others leadership was more distributed throughout the team. Even more confounding, two teams could be composed of many of the same team members and yet differ greatly in their effectiveness. Basically, it seemed as though the individuals composing the team mattered little.

In the end, the Aristotle project concluded, in the words of Google analyst Julia Rozovsky "*Who* is on a team matters less than how the team members interact, structure their work, and view their contributions."[42]

Google's study found that successful teams had *structure and clarity*, coming from clear goals, roles, and action plans. This highlights the importance of building shared goals and action plans early in the formation stage, as we've discussed.

They also found that individuals in successful teams felt their work had *impact* and *meaning*. They believed their work mattered and were doing things that they each found important. This emphasizes how important it is to share with your team the *why* of the work being done, as well as celebrating the results accomplished and showing their importance in terms of how they're benefiting society and others, and not just in monetary terms.

Finally, they found that successful teams had high *dependability*, the team members counted on each other to do quality work on time. And most important of all, successful teams scored high in *psychological safety*, a trait that seemed to underpin all the rest.

Psychological safety and group norms

Psychological safety can be defined in a team setting, as "sense of confidence that the team will not embarrass, reject, or punish someone for speaking up."[43]

Think back to a time when you felt completely lost in a team meeting because you didn't understand what the goal was or you weren't clear about a key concept. Did you speak up and ask about it? Or did you think speaking up would make you look stupid and out of the loop? Did you just keep quiet and decided to look it up by yourself later or ask someone individually?

In many settings, most of us will choose the latter option, keeping quiet and finding things out by ourselves. But this shifts when we're in a team with high psychological safety. Then we don't mind asking "stupid" questions or risk looking uninformed, unaware, or naïve.

Psychological safety allows for interpersonal risk-taking. It's a common concept in counselling and psychological first aid, where the first goal is to establish a psychological (and of course physical) safe space. This allows for emotions to emerge in a contained setting. Now new research in the workplace is showing that psychological safety also fosters creativity and success in our teams.

So how do we build a psychologically safe space? The degree of psychological safety in a team largely depends on something that has intrigued the management and organizational behaviour researchers for many years: group norms.

Group norms are the unwritten or written rules that govern a team. Its "standards of conduct," so to speak. Whether they are openly acknowledged or not, group norms exist in every team and have a powerful influence on group behaviour. These rules can be established and enforced proactively, in an open and participatory way. But if they are not, they will *still* be established, albeit in a more subconscious manner.

Stop for a minute to think about your family or a group of friends. What are your group's norms? Is it OK to criticize? To speak loudly, shout, or swear? Is there an unspoken agreement about who's the jester and who the subject of the jokes? When you plan a get-together, does everyone bring something to eat or drink without this having to be discussed? The same happens in our work teams. Norms get established.

Group norms help explain why you can be in two teams composed of many of the same individuals, but one team has a great, positive vibe and everybody speaks up and shares, while the other is dull and grey, criticism is heavy and people tend to attack each other. Different group norms can create varying levels of psychological safety in a team.

So the first step to creating psychological safety in your team is being upfront about the norming process that happens in any group. As we've seen, the norming phase is an expected phase any team will go through, and this is where group norms get formed. Proactively managing that process and being upfront with your team on the reasons why this is important, can lead to better group norms that allow for the emergence of a psychologically safe space.

Many of the issues in this book have to do with you, as a leader, setting the foundations on which to build healthy group norms in your team: being humble, active listening, caring for people as people. Research has pointed to other key things you can add to this foundation specifically to build up psychological safety in your team.

Shift the focus to learning

According to Amy Edmondson, the Novartis Professor of Leadership and Management at Harvard Business School, in order to foster psychological safety, it's important to "frame the work as a learning problem, not an execution problem."[44]

Of course, we all want to get great results and avoid mistakes, but a relentless focus on accountability without psychological safety can result in mistakes not being shared, and thus, missed opportunities for improvement.

These issues have been studied extensively in high-risk settings, such as hospital wards or airplane cockpits, where mistakes in a medical dose or a flight decision could cost human lives. Studies show that building psychological safety allows people to share their mistakes and *also* point out the mistakes their hierarchical superiors are making. Just imagine a nurse not daring to point out to a tired doctor that he's got the medication dose wrong or a co-pilot not daring to point out a mistake to the pilot and you'll see why psychological safety can be key.

By openly acknowledging that mistakes will happen at some point due to the degree of uncertainty and interdependence in the team, you can set the basis for more open communication, with people more confident to ask questions and share and point out mistakes. This, in turn, can allow for immediate corrective actions, or for learning from mistakes, which will, in turn, improve the performance of the team.

One great way of doing this is by establishing a "lessons-learned" conversation at the end of each milestone or goal, or routinely in each weekly meeting. This conversation can be set up by using three quick questions: a) What went well? b) What could have gone better? and c) How do we ensure we do better next time?

Ensure everybody gets a chance to speak up

Other research has shown that successful teams have what researchers call "equality of distribution of conversational turn-taking." This means that, *at the end of the day*, all team members participated roughly equally; even though, for some assignments or parts of the meeting, some members would remain more silent than others.

Equal distribution of conversation can clearly be established as a group norm. You as a leader can enhance it by modelling it and explicitly encouraging people to speak up and to listen respectfully. You can train yourself and your team in good listening skills. You can also foster it by appointing moderators to all meetings who are specifically tasked with making sure everybody gets heard out. You can talk individually to your team members to encourage them to speak up more often or listen up more often, according to their personalities.

Model fallibility and curiosity

Dr Edmondson also suggests modelling the traits you wish to foster on your team.[45] Be the first one to acknowledge your own mistakes, limitations, and uncertainties. We've talked about acknowledging mistakes more extensively in Chapter 4 on being responsible. As for acknowledging your limitations and uncertainties, an easy way of modelling this is to create a habit of asking your team two questions after exposing an idea or plan of action: What am missing here? Which part did I get wrong?

To model curiosity in learning, ask lots of questions about your own work and that of your team members. Make sure to frame these questions as thoughtful inquiry and not destructive criticism. Model giving positive feedback first. Routinely ask for other people's thoughts. Make sure to moderate meetings in such a way that questions do not become destructive or personal. Show a passion for learning and hunting down ways to improve the work.

Foster social sensitivity in your team

Researchers have shown that successful teams also have a high "average social sensitivity."[46] Teams with high social sensitivity are good at perceiving how individual members feel based on body language, facial expressions, tones of voice, and other means. This awareness helps in creating a psychologically safe space, as people are more aware and sensitive towards each other.

Social sensitivity can also be enhanced by group norms that foster respect, listening, and caring for other people, and you can, of course, model it yourself in your individual and team interactions.

Taken together, this research on successful teams is very

encouraging, especially for those of us who have no hiring and firing power over our team members. We may not be able to influence team composition, but the key characteristics of successful teams are things over which we *do* have control. We can provide clarity and meaning for the work being done and establish healthy group norms that increase dependability and psychological safety.

* * *

In this chapter, we've laid out the stages of team formation and discussed how you can support the building of a successful team.

The process starts with getting to know your team members better at an individual level. We've discussed why this is important for you as a leader and the benefits it can bring, not only in gaining clarity but also in gaining the trust of your team.

We then followed the process of how individuals go from a group of people to a team. Understanding this process keeps you from despairing when the storming phase sets in, as you know it'll pass and will only move you closer to success. We also analysed strategies you can use at each stage to manage this process more effectively, ultimately helping your team onwards to the performing stage.

Finally, we talked about what research can teach us about the characteristics of successful teams and how you can foster these characteristics in your team, starting from the forming stage, by modelling the traits you wish to see and making sure you establish healthy group norms for psychological safety.

Forming your team is your first challenge as a leader, but your tasks don't end when your team is performing well. No matter how strong and effective teams are, communication problems and conflicts *will* arise, as this is natural in any human relationship. In the next chapters, we discuss how you can set up, from the beginning, strong communication strategies. In the last section of the book, we will delve deeper into how to manage conflict.

CHAPTER 8
COMMUNICATION AND ITS CHALLENGES

COMMUNICATION is the one single issue that makes or breaks teams. Communication is one of the hardest challenges for teams and organizations, and even for many of us, as individuals in our personal lives. In this chapter we'll first discuss the communication process, and analyse all the places where this apparently simple process can go wrong, as well as the basic tools of effective communication aimed at building trust and cohesion in a team. In the next chapter, we will move on to propose specific informal and formal communication strategies that, depending on your setting, may be important for you and your team to have.

THE COMMUNICATION PROCESS

The communication process has been defined as "the transmission of information and the exchange of meaning between at least two people."[47] The main thing you should take from this is that, in any communication, both information *and* meaning are exchanged. This is usually at the core of many miscommunications.

The communication process, at its most simple, involves a

transmitter, a message, and a receiver.[48] The transmitter or sender, Person A, codes or packs the information into a message (step 1). In order to do this, the information is passed through the person's perceptual filters. The message is sent through a communication channel (face to face, email, text message) to the receiver (step 2). Person B, the receiver, then decodes this message, passing it through his or her own perceptual filters, to obtain the information and the meaning (step 3).

This simple model allows us to understand why communication tends to be so problematic; it's inherently an error-prone process! It has two steps involving coding and decoding of information, which are both subject to human perceptions and assumptions.

Coding and decoding

In the *coding* of the message, the sender chooses words and how the message will be expressed (e.g., loudly, softly, angrily). We choose--not always consciously--what information to share and what to withhold. The message passes through the perceptual filters of the sender, who is also in a particular environment that gives context and meaning to the message. Think of what it means to say, "It's hot today," when it's a sunny morning in the middle of the winter, and it's 8°C instead of the usual -15°C. As opposed to saying, "It's hot today," when you're on a tropical beach and it's 40°C instead of 32°C.

For a message to be successfully transmitted, the **decoding** of it has to be accurate. The receiver has to correctly understand the words chosen and the way the message was expressed.

But we do not receive information passively, we interpret it based on our own **context** and **perceptual filters**, our beliefs, motives, biases, prejudices, assumptions, and emotions. These all may all interfere with accurate decoding of the message. Our perceptual filters and own context affect which part of the message we hear, or we decide to focus on, and how we interpret it.

We can help our message to be correctly decoded by taking care, when we're coding it, to tailor the message to our audience and think about their context.

To help me think about how messages get coded and decoded, I like to use the concept of "metadata." If you know a bit about spreadsheets or databases, you'll have heard the word before.

Say you have a simple spreadsheet with three columns, one with names of your team members, another with their birthday, and a third with their salary. The obvious content is the data inside your cells. This is the information that you are consciously wanting to transmit.

Metadata is the information *about* the data. The metadata in this spreadsheet file comprises, for example, information about what each cell should look like (e.g., a date format, a text format, or a monetary format), or information about the whole spreadsheet such as the file name, who created it and at what time.

When we share the spreadsheet file with someone, we normally do so because we want them to see the data it contains (e.g., the names and birthdays and salaries). We rarely stop to think about the metadata we are sharing as well.

Similarly, we can think of messages as having metadata. The metadata in our messages will include everything that we share unintentionally: verbal cues such as tone of voice and inflections, hand signs and body language as well as facial expressions. Metadata also includes our context and our perceptual filters, things we normally tend to forget to share explicitly (e.g., when you say "it's hot today," whether you are in a snowy mountaintop or on a tropical beach).

Next time you are sending a message, stop for a moment and

think if you message has any important metadata and whether you're making it explicit. What's the context? Is the situation urgent? Are you worried? Where is this coming from? Are you transmitting this with a smile or a frown? Are you being inadvertently dismissive in your gestures?

The communication channel

Coding and decoding are key, but the **communication channel** is also important and may also facilitate or hinder communication. Communication channels vary in the amount of context they can share and the speed at which we receive **feedback** from the receiver as the message is being decoded.

Compare for example a face-to-face message, where both you and the receiver are in the same room and the receiver can read your facial expressions and body language, against a quick text message, where you have less metadata (facial expressions, body language, tone of voice, shared context) to help the receiver understand the message and the transmitter figure out quickly whether the message was understood correctly or not. It's no coincidence that emoji have become so commonplace in text messages. They provide a tiny bit of this much-needed emotional context.

In summary, the sender needs to find ways of conveying important contextual information to the receiver. The receiver must remember, upon decoding, that decoding can go wrong. He or she must pay attention to any perceptual filters and consider that she or he has a limited amount of contextual information.

COMMON COMMUNICATION CHALLENGES

Understanding how a message is "packaged" by the sender, shared, and then "unpackaged" by the receiver, helps us visualize and work through common types of communication challenges.

Message issues

Choice of words. This pertains to the message itself. We've all been there at some point. A poor choice of words or a careless comment can easily create a communication problem. The context and the communication channel can both have an impact on our choice of words. When we are under pressure we tend to be more careless, for example. When we choose a written communication channel, we normally have more time to choose our words.

Too much or too little information. Mark had just started working for a large global travel company when the results of an employee satisfaction survey were released. In his department, his predecessor had scored the lowest in the area of communication with his team. Mark was confused because his predecessor appeared to be constantly emailing his team members.

After asking around, though, he concluded that the problem may have actually been communication overload. His predecessor had sent out *too many* emails to busy employees, who became oblivious to them.

Mark decided to try something different--a simple daily slideshow update with what was happening that day, project reminders, sales results, process changes, and even motivational quotes. He went for graphics, gifs, and a colourful presentation, keeping text to a minimum. He made sure the content was highly targeted to the audience. More importantly, he created ownership for the slideshow by giving the team access to the document so they could contribute anything they wanted to communicate too.

Every day, at 10am, he uploaded the daily update to the company's internal social networking site. The initial response was guarded but within a couple of weeks the team would become agitated if the upload was even five minutes late. Mark and the other managers also noticed that the staff was much more aware of what was going on than before. A year later, on the employee satisfaction survey, the same communication question received a 100% satisfaction score.

It is fairly obvious how too little information can lead to communication breakdowns. People can feel left out of the loop or just won't have enough information to act on.

As we saw from Mark's story, however, too much information can also be an issue. His predecessor had been pelting his team with emails, and still, the team evaluated communication as low. In Mark's case, the previous manager had been sharing too much information that wasn't targeted at the specific audience, so that after a while it became just background noise, *and they still felt communication was poor.*

Your team is busy too. Avoid bombarding them with emails or meetings. Don't pop up every minute to talk to them.

The communication systems we'll propose later will help you create a balance between too much and too little communication. But you should continue to ask for feedback, as the communication needs can change. For instance, newcomers might need more information than old-timers or, in times of stress or rapid change, information might need to be shared more often and probably more succinctly.

Context issues

Lack of, limited or un-relatable context. Here the sender isn't providing specific enough "metadata" in her message for us to decode it correctly. When an issue is emotionally charged, lack of context for understanding where the emotional charge is coming from (or even that there is one) usually leads to serious communication challenges.

For example, you ask Jack to help you out by creating a simple inventory of documents that could be used by the whole team.

Jack answers furiously back that creating inventories isn't part of his job description. For the life of you, you can't fathom why he would get so worked up about such a simple thing until a later conversation reveals that that filing and inventorying was his sole task in his previous job and he vowed to get away from such tasks.

Problems can also happen when the metadata shared is not specific enough, leading to different interpretations. For example, Andrea asks you to provide a document saying, "It isn't urgent." Not urgent for you might mean it can be left until next month while not urgent for her might mean she can wait until tomorrow morning.

Perceptual filter issues

Misreading of a message. This involves a misunderstanding of the things we share in the message due to the perceptual filters of the receiver. Here the decoding of the message goes wrong. Our perceptual filters can lead us to hear something that wasn't said or miss something that was said.

Misunderstandings can happen because of what we share *explicitly* (e.g., verbally or in writing) but also what we share *inadvertently* (e.g., body language and facial expressions, tone of voice). As primates, we are incredibly adept at non-verbal communication. Your brain receives more signals from another person's face gestures and body language than those you're conscious of. Some researchers suggest humans can use and read up to twenty-one different facial expressions, and we potentially read fleeting involuntary micro-expressions as well.[49]

This reading of non-verbal cues is normally very useful for allowing us to successfully navigate social interactions. But sometimes it can backfire if we misread the message.

We've all had experiences like this: I present a proposal to, say, Karen. When I ask her what she thinks, she sighs, looks to the floor, crosses her arms, and finally says, "Yes, we could do that." Even though Karen's accepting my proposal, I go away with the impression that she didn't like it. When I ask her about it later, she seems surprised. "Oh no," she says. "I thought it was a very good proposal. I was already thinking forward as to how to implement it!" What I read as disinterest was in fact distraction because she was thinking ahead.

Channel issues

Choice of communication channel. Using the wrong communication channel for a particular communication can also lead to problems. One common mistake is using email or a text message to talk about a delicate matter or to share a message that may elicit strong emotions. Not having the other person physically in front of you prevents you from reading their body language and facial expressions and, as such, you may miss important feedback cues.

On the opposite side, we sometimes choose face-to-face or telephone communication for highly-detailed messages or instructions that would benefit from written support. Say, I'm chatting with Sheila in the hallway, and I remember I need her to do something. Right away, I launch into a detailed description of what needs to be done. If Sheila doesn't take notes, chances are good she'll forget half the steps. I may get mad at her, but I could've prevented the situation by sending an email instead, or afterward as further support, so that Sheila could read my instructions as many times as needed.

By understanding these common sources of communication challenges, we can think of how to work around them to improve communication with our team.

TOOLS FOR EFFECTIVE COMMUNICATION

For any communication exchange, be it face to face, verbal or written, one-on-one, or in a team meeting, there are a series of strategies you can use to optimize your exchanges:

Choose your communication channel

The amount of metadata that gets shared inadvertently isn't the same in all channels of communication, meaning some channels are more appropriate than others for different types of communication.

Face-to-face messages have the highest inadvertent sharing of metadata. The receiver is in the same environment as you, the sender, which can help prevent some context-related miscommunications. You are both able to read each other's face and body language clearly. You also have instant feedback, both conscious and subconscious, and this back and forth allows for any misunderstanding to be caught in time and dissipated more quickly. Any communication that requires quick turnaround and feedback (e.g., brainstorming, reaching a consensus) is better tackled face-to-face. Emotionally charged or delicate matters (a raise, a review, something that the person is not doing well) can also benefit from face-to-face communication.

Video-messages. After face-to-face communication come video-messages (e.g., teleconferences, skype, facetime, and so on), where you aren't in the same room with the person, but you can still see his or her facial expressions. In a voice call, you have some input from voice inflections, although rarely with the same high fidelity as in true face-to-face conversations. Video also allows for quick feedback to verify correct message decoding.

The rise of virtual work environments has made video-communication commonplace. Video calls can indeed provide a lot of value, but keep in mind your ability to read facial expressions and body language will be worse than in true face-to-face communication.

Telephone or voice messages. Here voice nuances may provide some additional metadata, but you'll lack visual cues from facial expressions or body language. Because they're still back and forth communications, phone conversations do make detecting incorrect decoding quicker and help solve potential misunderstandings.

If we're working with someone long distance, our choices may come down to telephone or email. If feedback and discussion are needed, telephone communication normally allows you to sort out the problem faster.

Written messages. Written messages (emails and text messages) have no voice inflections or visual cues to help interpretation and have a longer feedback time. A lot of metadata may be missing, and the receiver may not know whether your angry, sad, joking, dead serious, or desperate. Phrases that can be made to sound lighter with a voice inflection or a smile may come out sounding accusatory or negative in writing. Without voice inflections and facial expressions, sarcasm and joking are harder to detect.

Written messages, however, are useful for recording agreements and thought processes that need to be accessed later. They're effective for sharing factual information or instructions, where the receiver may need to refer back to the information later on.

Visual messages (graphs, figures). In some cases, such as sharing factual information, graphs, figures, images, or other visualizations can be an even better choice than written words. In Mark's case study, discussed above, his predecessor's emails probably didn't get read, but the team appreciated the graphs and gifs shared in the daily power-point Mark set up. Visual information can be consumed faster, and studies show that graphs or images are remembered much better than written words.[50] Visual messages are not, however, protected from perceptual filters and decoding issues. They can carry a lot of metadata, so you'll need to take care when preparing them to ensure they're interpreted appropriately.

Prepare yourself beforehand

Once you've decided on the best communication channel to use, the next step is to proactively prepare your message. Being prepared is especially important for key messages or difficult communications. Whenever you have a difficult conversation on your schedule, you may want to do a short exercise I like to call my "pre-meeting cheat sheet." You can also use a similar exercise for preparing a more formal presentation or even an email.

Grab a piece of paper and in three to five minutes, brainstorm, in writing, the following points:

1. **What do you want to say?** First, determine your *key message*. If communications get tangled and you can only transmit one message, which one will it be? Then, make a list of sub-points or additional messages in order of importance. If you have more than three key issues, can you move some to another occasion? With this list, when you start communicating, you'll be very clear on what you want to transmit.

2. **What would be a great outcome?** If you could will the meeting or communication exchange to go the way you wanted it to, what would the *end result* look like? What would be a home run? Do you want consensus or do you want a decision to be made no matter what? Do you want to motivate your team or come out with a strategy? For example, at a team meeting your home run could be "getting consensus on the new marketing strategy" or "creating cohesion in the team." At a first interview with

your new team member, it could be "making the new member feel welcome." At a presentation with donors, it may be "getting them to donate $100,000 per person to the new project."

3. **How do you want to say it?** Through a direct approach, i.e., just stating clearly your purpose and your why? Through an indirect approach, i.e., helping the individual(s) to reach the conclusion by themselves? Your strategy may vary depending on your outcome. If you want to ensure consensus, more discussion will be needed than if you want to just share facts or a decision you've made. If you're sharing a complex idea or strategy, can you use an example or an analogy for clarification and greater impact? If your aim is to get people on board, you may want to look at ways to inspire them.

4. **What is your intention for yourself?** Independent of how the exchange goes and whether or not you achieve your communication goal, you have control over how you'll feel before, during, and after the exchange. Be conscious of this control and your power to choose how you'll feel. For example, your intention can be "no matter what the other person says, I won't get angry." Or "I will strive to talk for only 20% of the time and use the other 80% to really listen." Or "I will bite my tongue before discarding any silly idea that John comes up with this time. I will write it down and try to consider it from his point of view."

You'll find a cheat sheet that you can use to prepare each of your exchanges beforehand in Clinic 17 in the Workbook.

Practice active listening

Now that you are clear on what you want to say, it's time to take a step back and focus on listening. Many of us equate communication with speaking, yet paradoxically, a key aspect of any productive communication is not how well we speak, but how well we listen.

My advice is simple. First, listen. Then, listen. Finally, listen some more. Of course, you'll come prepared and with your own agenda for this meeting. But you'll gain a lot by listening first and changing your mind if needed or sticking to your agenda but sharing it with the new understanding of the other person's viewpoint.

In most cases, when we think we're listening, in truth we're already preparing a response in our heads. Let go of this temptation to answer and solve the issue immediately and try to really focus on what the other person is saying, without jumping to conclusions.

Repeat what the other person has said back to them to check if you understood correctly what he or she was saying. This is called paraphrasing, and it's an incredibly useful technique. It also helps you focus your listening abilities, as you know you'll need to repeat the information back, and verify your understanding of what has been said. For example, say, "If I understand correctly, you're saying that..." "My feeling, from what I'm hearing, is that you are having trouble with _____. Is that correct?" "Are you saying that _____?"

When it comes to the other person feeling listened to, small things also matter. Make eye contact. Avoid crossing your arms. Keep your phone in your pocket, not on the table, and make sure it's on silent mode. Don't pick it up unless you're waiting for a truly urgent call.

Ask probing questions

When you think you're done with listening, you're ready to ask some open-ended questions and listen some more. Good probing questions make the other person (or people) feel you're paying attention and help them clarify the problem or brainstorm the solution.

For example, you can say, "What do you think is causing this?" "What are your ideas about how to solve this?" "What is the best approach for moving forward, in your view?" "What other paths have you considered?" "How can I help?"

Most of us normally try to jump in quickly to provide solutions, but this might not be the best approach if you really want to grow your team.

Share your viewpoint only if it's relevant

Now it's finally time to share your viewpoint *if this is still necessary and appropriate.* If you're in an individual or group meeting and the person or the team has already managed to find the solution or reach the outcome that was the ultimate goal for your meeting, then you don't need this step and you can move to close the exchange.

It is terribly tempting to share our viewpoint and explain our grand idea, but that's about ego, not great leadership. If your viewpoint can provide a different, alternate solution to the situation, help the other person or the team to consider other possibilities, or even create empathy by showing that you have been through this as well, it might be worth sharing it. If it will only reinforce what others have already said, it might not be necessary.

Talk from a personal perspective

If you do share your viewpoint, differentiate between your thoughts & perceptions and facts so everyone knows you're coming from a personal perspective. For example, say "I believe that the best solution is _____." Instead of "the best solution is _____."

Unless you can prove your solution is the best solution, for now this is a hypothesis, not fact. Saying "I think we could solve it this way," instead of "this is the way to solve it," implies there might be other ways to solve it, opens the way for discussion, and is less patronising.

This strategy also works to build bridges between what you think and what the other person said. "From what you've told me, my impression is that the problem lies here: _____. My suggestion would be to tackle it by _____."

Share negative feedback in a constructive way

If your end result is solving a degrading situation, pay attention to how you share negative feedback. While you might be tempted to vent your frustrations, remember this is much more likely to corner you in a dead end, not resolve the situation.

Strategies for giving negative feedback vary. To prevent being overly negative, some people share negative feedback first, followed by positive feedback. Others go from positive items to negative ones. Still, others use a sandwich approach: positive-negative-positive.

In a recent article, Adam Grant, organizational psychologist and author of *Give and Take* argues that the sandwich approach can be counterproductive,[51] as it can result in either the person ignoring the positive feedback or not giving enough weight to the negative one. So what other strategies can we use to make sure our negative feedback is well received?

- Turn the negatives around and share them as learning and growth opportunities. Grant cites a study in which feedback became more effective just by explaining beforehand to the individuals why this feedback was being shared. If we jump right in into criticising, chances are the other person will become defensive. Explaining that we're giving feedback because we care about the other person's growth and believe in them can change the perspective. For example, you could say "I want to share feedback on the last report because I believe this will allow you to do much better next time." To make this work, you need to follow the criticism with discussing a plan for doing things better next time and supporting your team member in any area where he or she might require help.

- Ask for permission to share the feedback. Grant argues that, by giving the person power over receiving the feedback and creating ownership, people become less defensive. Simply say you have some feedback you believe could help him or her do better next time and ask whether they'd like to hear it.

- Talk about the work, not about the person's skills. "You've been doing low-quality work" won't be as well received as "I have the impression that this report was not as good as previous ones." Criticising a task rather than the person opens the door to a discussion and helps avoid defensiveness.

- Be specific. It's not everything that the other person is doing wrong. Give one or two specific and recent examples (but avoid an unending list that will just destroy the other person's confidence). For example: "The last report you shared was delivered late and was lacking the section on new clients."

Be sensitive

If the person breaks down and explains to you that his or her terrible performance has been due to an impending divorce, don't try to follow through with your agenda. Let it go. Care about your people as people. Offer support and a listening ear. Find a time later for another talk, when the storm has calmed down, where you can get back to your agenda.

Close with a call to action

Whenever it's appropriate, reinforce your exchange with a call-to-action. Clarify with the other person what needs to happen next. Lead the other person to propose this next step, creating ownership of it. Then close the exchange by stating in two phrases what has been agreed, the times, and date for the next exchange, if appropriate.

* * *

Strong communication is key for a successful team. Understanding the communication process allows us to see more clearly where communication challenges lie, and all the ways where the process can go wrong.

From this understanding, we can build a set of general tools to improve our communication ability as leaders with our teams, and within and outside our organizations. These general tools for constructive communication can be incorporated into your communication approach with your team, which benefits from including both informal and formal communication strategies. We will look at these in the next chapter.

CHAPTER 9

TEAM COMMUNICATION STRATEGIES

SONIA was a technician at a research group where I worked years ago. She was undoubtedly highly-skilled technically. But with time I came to grasp where she provided the real added value to our group. She was a bit of a chatterbox, and an outsider would have wrongly labelled her a gossip. In fact, probably completely unbeknownst to her, she was a connector, someone who relays information.

She would chat up all of us while working, in the hallway, or at lunch. She was a great listener, and it was easy to open up to her. But I learned to be cautious because, unless you expressly told her to not share a piece of information, she would probably share it with others. It would be unfair to say she talked behind our backs because she would have said exactly the same things had any of us been present. She didn't spew lies or criticism. She just shared honestly, naively, and in good faith, information that each of the members of the team had shared with her.

At first, this made me highly uncomfortable. I used to be very reserved and rarely shared personal information with bosses or colleagues who I didn't consider friends. But little by little I came to appreciate how she connected us all with her openness and information sharing. I came to rely on her to understand why the boss was on edge that day, why one of my colleagues was behind on a project, what was happening in the other research groups down the hall, and who to talk to if I needed a particular piece of equipment.

Her impressive communication abilities, which she probably didn't even know she possessed, her naiveté when sharing information, her good heart and openness made us a more cohesive team, helped us be more honest with each other and prevented conflict from simmering unchecked. If you were angry at someone, and Sonia found out, you knew you'd better own it up quickly and go talk to the person before she did. If you didn't, chances were the other person would find out and come talk to you about it anyway.

When we think about team communication, we tend to imagine meetings, memos, and minutes. Yet team communication comprises not only these formal strategies but also the informal communication strategies at which Sonia excelled. These informal strategies, the chatter that goes on in the background of a team and organization, are just as important as formal strategies such as meetings, performance evaluations, emails, and minutes. In this chapter, we will discuss both sets of strategies.

INFORMAL COMMUNICATION STRATEGIES

Use the hallway

In some Spanish-speaking countries, gossip in the office is called "radio pasillo," the hallway radio. As in, "Hey Tim, I heard on the hallway radio that you had a meeting with the engineering department last week?"

What this implies is that the hallway (and the water-cooler, the coffee machine, or the cafeteria) are places where people interact and communicate in informal ways. Sonia was a natural at taking advantage of these communication spaces. But you as a leader can also learn to leverage informal communication opportunities in your favour.

Let's be clear, I'm not talking about gossip here. Gossip is defined in the dictionary as "casual or unconstrained conversation or reports about other people, typically involving details that are not confirmed as true." Gossiping, when it implies talking about other people behind their back in a negative way, is the opposite of a communication enhancing strategy. Informal "hallway chats," on the other hand, are a powerful tool to engage people directly in casual or unconstrained conversation to talk about *their own issues*.

Hallway chats, then, are short, friendly, informal chats you have with your team members whenever an opportunity crops up. And you make it part of your schedule to *ensure that they crop up often*. You use them to talk about everything that is going on in their own agendas, yours, and the organization's.

- **Their life**. This is a great opportunity to apply the "care about the people as people" mindset. Ask about their weekend, their vacations, their evening, find out about their hobbies, favourite foods, books, TV programs, pets. Share some personal information of your own if you're asked, or as a prompt to keep the conversation flowing, but be sure to listen more than you talk.

- **Their work**. How's it going with their latest task or latest project? Have they encountered any stumbling blocks? What's going well? Do they like the new task? Can you facilitate anything? Make sure you avoid making these into accountability meetings. If they feel like accountability meetings for your team members, they'll start avoiding you. These are informal, friendly "how is it going?" moments. You're opening the door for them to come share milestones and stumbling blocks with you, so projects don't get stalled.

- **Organization news.** This is you doing the talking for once. Use "hallway chats" to share information not important enough to be included in a meeting, but that your team members may still feel better about hearing. We all like to be in the loop. Let your team members know how your meeting with the other department or with the boss went. Pass on any news from the organization or ideas you've been mulling.

Set up your office to enhance good communication

When Laura started her new team leader position, she made it clear to her team that she was instating an open door policy. People should feel free to come to her office at any time and talk to her. Good communication was high on her priority list. People made use of the open door policy, and she received them informally in her office many times.

When the time for the quarterly evaluation came up, however, anonymous surveys showed that her team didn't consider communication with her to be the best. Surprised, she did some more digging.

She found out that her office setting was sabotaging her communication strategy. When people came to her office, a desk sat between her and them and on the desk was her computer. People felt she was only partly paying attention to them because her computer was still open and an object of her attention.

Realizing the problem, Laura reorganized her office. She put her desk (and computer) at the back against the wall and set up a small round table with spare chairs at the front. Whenever someone came in, she would swivel her desk chair to join the small round table and sit with her team member in a computer-clean, paper-clean context.

If you're serious about enhancing communication with your team, make sure your environment helps instead of hinders your efforts. Ask yourself these questions. When people come in, is your back turned toward them? Or can you see them immediately and greet them warmly? Do they have a space to sit down to talk? Is this space (chair or bench) clean of clutter or do they have to start by clearing away ten kilos of files to sit down? Is there a partition (a wide desk for example or a computer) between where you sit and where they sit? Do you make sure there are no distractions competing for your attention (computer, telephone, tablet) when they come in to talk to you? Find ways to tweak your office space to make it more inviting and enhance rather than inhibit, informal communication.

My old boss had a good strategy to lure people into his office. He had an espresso machine in there. Many of us coffee addicts would pay him a visit just to get a coffee and then stay two to three minutes to chat. Candy jars can also work wonders. Install a transparent jar of candy, chocolates, or cookies in a prominent and easily accessible spot in your office. Make sure it's always full and invite people to come in and get some candy when the door is open. This gives an excuse for people to drop by your office without a clear agenda and allows you to engage them in some informal chit-chat.

Clarify your open door policy

While open door policies might be good for communication, full-time open door policies can hurt your own creative work and productivity. It is important to find a balance to allow yourself to do your work and circumscribe your management time. A good balance can be achieved by an "always open door for urgent matters" policy combined with a specific period of time every day where you are always available for your team for non-urgent matters (e.g., 11am to 2pm). This time compartment coincides with the time you're allocating in your daily planning to management time. Whatever your policy is, make sure to communicate it clearly to your team and clarify what constitutes an urgent matter, including personal ones.

If you have an open door policy, make sure you're truly and readily available to your team during that time. It is frustrating for team members if they come in to talk to you and you make them wait for twenty minutes. Their time is just as valuable as yours, and it's important to respect that.

When they come in, drop whatever else you are doing and greet them warmly. If you're in the middle of something important, say another conversation or call, smile and ask if they could come back in ten minutes or you'll come look for them. And then follow up on that promise.

Use lunches abundantly

Don't skip lunch. When I first started as a team leader, I stopped going to the cafeteria. I was sure the people on my team would resent me if I cut into their "free" time by inserting myself into their cafeteria table. While your team may appreciate some team-leader-free time and you should definitely create that space for them, lunches can be used in a zillion more productive ways than just working at your desk.

Use your lunchtime to talk to people. You could, for instance, invite team members informally to a one-on-one or small group lunch once in a while. (Make sure everybody gets a turn, though.) You can have lunch with people in other teams, other departments, your boss, or such.

This is prime communication time. It's not a working lunch but an informal opportunity to get to know people better. It can pay huge dividends later, creating opportunities for collaboration, and enlarging and solidifying your network.

Many successful people make it a habit to get to know a least one new person in their organization per week. They use the lunch hour to build their network, and you can too.

Provide regular informal feedback

The first rule about feedback is don't wait until it's too late to give it. If you are already considering firing a person, then it's too late. If a team member isn't performing well, the first thing you should consider is whether you've given him or her adequate and timely feedback.

Imagine you sit down with your team leader or your boss in December for an annual performance evaluation. Your boss lets you know that the quality of the reports you've been giving each quarter is not as good as it should be. Astonished, you look at her and ask, "Well, why didn't you tell me this after I handed in the very first report in March?! I would have had three additional opportunities of making it better!"

One of the reasons so-called performance evaluations or appraisals are heavily criticised (apart from the numerous biases they may have) is that in many organizations they happen only once a year. Thus, employees miss many opportunities for growth and improvement.

Giving and receiving feedback can be hard, which is why as team leaders, we normally avoid giving it until it's requested at these annual evaluations. Yet, if you manage to create solid formal and informal communication with your team, build trust, and establish a growth mindset, you'll be able to provide informal feedback regularly without causing stress or resentment for either party.

The benefits of informal feedback are many. First, it can be provided immediately after an event (e.g., preparing a report, giving a presentation, organizing an event, dealing with a difficult client or beneficiary), when both you and your team member still have the details fresh in your minds, allowing for a more accurate analysis. Second, if it's for an activity that will be repeated, it gives your team member the opportunity to correct their course for the next time. Last, it makes formal biannual or annual feedback sessions easier, as you can go over improvements your team member has gained because of informal feedback. This is better than having to go over a long list of accumulated issues where your team member could do better next time, which is bound to create pressure and resentment.

FORMAL COMMUNICATION STRATEGIES

Your formal communication tools come in different flavours, with two common ones being meetings--either individual, group or subgroup meetings--and emails and memos, that is, talking and writing. These two strategies are not opposite but complementary, and they both may have a place in your formal communication system.

The components I find valuable in such a system include:

A structure for each team and individual meeting in your system

Establishing a structure includes knowing exactly what happens before, during, and after a meeting. Determine beforehand how the agenda for the meeting is developed and who develops it. Create a template for conducting regular meetings that can be used most of the time. For example, sharing successes first, then challenges, then a plan of action for the next inter-meeting period. Have a system in place for recording and sharing the meeting information among the team (e.g., minutes sent by email or a shared minutes folder in the cloud or both). Make sure everyone in your team knows these structural components.

A pre-meeting cheat sheet

This pre-meeting cheat sheet, which I introduced in Chapter

8, is a three- to five-minute exercise you can do before a meeting to ensure you're on top of things and crystal-clear on what you want to achieve. Your cheat sheet prompts you to answer three questions:

1. What's my main message and what's the best way to transmit it?

2. If I can achieve only one thing in this meeting, what would that be?

3. How do I want to act and feel during and after the meeting?

A cheat-sheet is particularly important for stressful or difficult meetings. Clinic 17 in the Workbook contains a Cheat Sheet template that you can print out.

Routine team meetings

Use routine team meetings to report on activities, stumbling blocks, successes, and agree on next steps, milestones, and deadlines. While how often these meetings take place will vary according to your specific team needs, it is important to:

- Make them regular. Meetings benefit from a fixed schedule, as it's easier for people to develop the habit of attending the meeting if they always happen at the same time.

- Ensure everybody knows they're expected to be there and why this is important.

- Ensure they happen often enough that the team spirit can be maintained and nurtured and there's a good flow of information (weekly or monthly meetings are good in some settings, but some teams need shorter bi-weekly or even daily meetings if things are moving fast).

Regular individual meetings

Scheduling regular individual meetings allows you to catch up with each of your team members and address any individual challenges they're going through, as well as give informal feedback. Make sure you have a clear agenda for this meeting as well and that your team member knows the agenda. It is important to leave enough flexibility to address things not listed on the agenda that may come up.

Use these individual meetings to coach your team member, address specific concerns, unblock problems, provide informal feedback or teach (or learn!) a new skill. The need for individual meetings may not be the same for each of your team members. Some people require weekly meetings, while others may be happy with catching up with you once every month.

Quarterly, biyearly or yearly reviews

Quarterly, bi-yearly, or yearly meetings are focused on giving and receiving feedback in a more formal manner. They're more akin to performance evaluations and not to be used for talking about daily work. Your organization may already use official performance evaluations or yearly appraisals. If you like these and agree to how they're structured, you can use them. If you don't like them or your organization doesn't have them, you can always create your own strategy for formal feedback and use it independently or in a complementary form to the ones favoured by your organization.

As we discussed above, feedback can and should be given informally. However, regular, expected and planned formal meetings with the sole purpose of giving and receiving feedback are also important. Because they have a set date, they allow both you and your team members to take the time to stop and analyse what's working and what could be improved. Also, formal meetings are an important motivational and planning tool, as they let both sides know how much has already been achieved and what remains to be accomplished. They also let you identify the not-so-evident obstacles that may be hindering your team members' effectiveness and professional growth.

In a long-term review, I believe it is important to analyse and discuss both areas of achievements and areas of opportunities.

Sharing both positive and negative aspects can work quite well, as long as everyone understand that this feedback is an opportunity for growth, and the feedback exercise is mutual. As a team leader you not only give feedback but also receive it, modelling this growth mindset and openness for critique.

The structure I like to follow for these formal feedback meetings is one that I learned from an advisor many years ago:

1. Goals accomplished and unplanned achievements
2. Goals not accomplished
3. Areas of strengths
4. Areas of opportunities
5. Next steps

You'll find a template for this review in Clinic 18 in the Workbook.

Let's work through this structure with an example. Imagine you are reviewing Tomomi:

Prepare for this meeting. Reserve half an hour before your formal evaluation meeting. Take out Tomomi's past performance evaluation and review the goals you set out together for this period. Do your own appraisal of which goals he's accomplished and think about what other unplanned goals he has achieved. Which goals weren't accomplished? Do you know why these weren't achieved? Write down your notes.

Then think about Tomomi's strengths, in particular those you think were most on display during the period or which he'd agreed to work on. Is he a team player? Is he great with clients or beneficiaries? Is he reliable? Is he efficient in his work? Does he contribute to creating a good atmosphere? Come up with at least one specific example for each of the strengths you have listed.

Go on to the areas of opportunity that you had both agreed upon in the last meeting. Which have improved and how? Make sure you have concrete examples. For instance: Last time you agreed that Tomomi would work more on sharing his ideas in meetings. He has indeed participated in almost every meeting this last period, and as you recall, a couple of months ago he shared a particularly powerful proposal on how to systematize contacts with the clients.

Think about new areas of opportunity and training you think may benefit Tomomi and write them out. Make sure you've done this homework before the meeting.

At the review meeting. As always, start the meeting by explaining the purpose of it and the structure you'll follow, and ask if the person is OK with it, adding you'll give them space at the end for any other issues he or she wants to discuss.

Go on to **review the concrete goals** that you and Tomomi had set for the period. First let Tomomi tell you what he thinks are the period's achievements. Add any you wrote down which he hasn't mentioned. Some people have a hard time recognizing their own achievements so make sure to point these out to them. Ask Tomomi about any achievements that weren't originally planned, and then add your own to the ones he lists.

From here, **move on to unaccomplished goals**. Ask the person what other goals he or she believes may not have been achieved. Discuss the reasons for this.

If you have some of your own, add them in a non-blaming way by saying, "What about your goal to complete the report for the donor?" Or "I believe another goal that wasn't reached was the proposal for a new training. What do you think?"

Also, make sure to do a reality check on any goals that Tomomi thinks he's achieved but you don't believe he's made enough progress in. You need to have concrete examples for this disagreement as well.

It's important that you recognize that external challenges and barriers may have kept your team member from completing a goal. But you should also ensure that the person takes responsibility for anything else that she or he could've done to get past those barriers.

To start a positive discussion about this subject, ask, "Is there anything that, in retrospect, you think you could've done to tackle these challenges?" Asking for help or notifying you of the challenges is also an area that can be explored.

Move on to strengths. Ask Tomomi to share what he thinks are his strongest assets and why. Prompt him to give examples. If your list of Tomomi strengths matches his list, then add your own specific examples, as a way of supporting what he's saying. If you've listed additional strengths, you can say, for instance, "I also think one of your strengths is conflict resolution. I saw you the other day at the team meeting, how you picked up on the tension between Tim and Sally and you diffused it before it escalated."

This is why your preparation time included thinking about specific examples. These are powerful.

Go on to **explore areas of opportunity**. First, ask Tomomi which areas he'd like to improve in. Be positive and supportive about the person's stated areas of opportunity. If they differ from the ones you brainstormed, gently ask what Tomomi thinks of these areas and give specific supporting examples.

For instance, you could say, "I've noticed that you've been much more consistent this period at bringing up and sharing your own ideas at meetings. I think it might be a good to keep building up on that by continuing to strengthen your public speaking skills. For example, at the last meeting with the client, I thought that a stronger structure would have helped you share your idea for their website in a more compelling way. What do you think? Would this be of interest to you?"

From areas of opportunity, you can naturally **move on to next steps.** Ask Tomomi about his goals for the next period and suggest the ones you've written down. Include any new training and courses he'd like to take. Make sure you explore hard skills (e.g., social media, marketing, statistics, CME courses), and soft skills (e.g., communication, time-management). Write down opportunities you agree on and concrete ways in which Tomomi will go about these, including any commitments you are making to help him.

Finally, **ask the person to reciprocate** and share candidly with you what's working well in your relationship with him, and also with the team in general. Ask for specific examples. Thank Tomomi. But other than that just be present and accept these comments. Don't try to explain yourself, justify your actions, or minimize their importance. Accepting praise graciously is just as important as giving praise.

Then ask him to share what he considers to be **your areas of opportunity** and give specific examples of things that could work better. Ask for clarifications if needed. Maintain your neutrality and accept the critique. Again, don't try to explain yourself, justify your actions, or minimize their importance.

You don't necessarily have to agree, but you do need to listen openly. Write them down, thank him for sharing this, and let him know you'll think some more about it (if you disagree) or that you'll brainstorm on ways to improve in these areas (if you agree).

For instance, if you agree with Tomomi when he says you forget to transmit important information to the whole team, you could show your understanding by saying, "I see what you mean. I think I did that same thing that day we met with the HR department, and I only told two people from the team the results of that meeting." A concrete example is worth a hundred words to prove you get it and you're able to identify your mistakes.

When you admit to mistakes, people will trust you to change.

Note down any agreements and commitments both of you make, plus the next date for a follow-up. Close the meeting on a good note. Send Tomomi the minutes and agreements from your meeting within twenty-four hours.

Types of team meetings

The group meeting is a great tool to keep everyone in the loop. In it your team can brainstorm ideas, reach consensus, problem-solve, maintain momentum and motivation, and foster team cohesion. But time lost to meetings is a regular complaint of both team members and management. Finding the right balance for meetings in your specific setting and adjusting it as the settings and your teams' needs change is important.

However, it is possible that despite your best efforts, some people will still complain about too few, too many, too long, or too short meetings! Remember needs may vary among your team members and it is not possible to satisfy everyone. In the end, it's your call.

Meetings can serve different purposes. You'll call different kinds of meetings depending on what you need to accomplish. Various methodologies exist for each type of meeting. You might want to look into what seems to work for your particular industry.

Progress meetings. You'll likely use progress meetings regularly. At a progress meeting, the team will update each other on their achievements, obstacles, and next steps. They'll ask for and receive support with challenges and moving forward.

Several methodologies for conducting this type of meeting have been developed. You may wish to read up on them to develop a system that works for your team. In the software development community, you might hear about the Agile methodology and Scrum or Kanban methods, for example, which can also work for other teams.

These methods might incorporate "stand-up" meetings, which are also common in hospitals, the military, restaurants, and other fast-paced environments. These are very short meetings (five to fifteen minutes) conducted regularly to succinctly report progress, distribute new tasks, and problem-solve. They aim to reduce time wasted by being stuck on a problem that could be quickly solved by someone else or by working on something that is no longer relevant. Because no one sits down, it helps in keeping the time short!

Information-sharing meetings. Here the aim is to transmit information to the audience. They can be used for presenting results, new methodologies, programmes, or technology proposals, as well as for teaching. They include presentations, panel debates, lectures, and similar. In many cases, they'll be more formal and use slides or video. Information-sharing meetings don't have to be unidirectional, with only the speaker contributing. You can engage the audience to speak or participate through their smartphones by using different apps.[52]

Decision-making meetings. These are normally used for more important decisions than the routine choices made during regular daily or weekly meetings. Different methodologies exist to conduct these, and you may want to look into them beforehand, especially for contentious decisions.

Participatory approaches, as well as individual or team brainstorming for the pros and cons of each proposed solution might be useful. In some cases, you might want to assign a particular person or pair the role of devil's advocate, to avoid bad decision making due to group-think.[53]

Creative meetings. These can happen at the start of a project or when you're faced with a particular problem. They can be used to find new ideas for products or programmes, or to design parts of an existing one (e.g. to come up with new ideas for workshops or create the contents of a particular workshop). They can also be used for problem-solving a specific obstacle (e.g. coming up with ways to cut costs, or solving a bottleneck in your flow of clients or beneficiaries). They benefit from the free-flow of ideas and a strong sense of psychological safety, where no proposals are rejected in their earlier stages, so that people feel comfortable sharing their boldest or craziest ideas.

Team building meetings. While all meetings have a team-building component, the goal of this particular type of meeting is not the work of the organization per se, but the team. You might use this kind of meeting at the beginning to help your team move faster from the forming and storming to the norming and performing stages. Later on, you can use them to keep growing your team, creating trust, cohesion, and efficient group work and maintaining healthy group norms. They can also be used when frictions arise, or to celebrate a win. Use participatory approaches and workshop-style exercises to bring your team together and solve any internal friction.

Conducting a team meeting

The first item when conducting a team meeting is to ensure your team has meeting guidelines, as we saw in Chapter 7. Clinic 16 in the Workbook provides a basis from which you can develop your own team's general meeting guidelines.

How you'll conduct a meeting will depend a large part on the type of meeting it is. However, certain general guidelines apply to a variety of meeting types.

Make sure invitations and reminders for the meeting (especially for a non-regular one) are sent sufficiently early. Make the most of your and your team's time by having a clear agenda for the meeting and, if appropriate, a strict schedule that everyone adheres to.

Use meetings to enhance the clarity and structure of tasks,

milestones, and goals, as well as the importance and meaning of the work being done. As we saw in the previous chapter, these items are important for effective teams.

Also use your team meetings to foster communication and reinforce positive group norms for your team, which we discussed in Chapter 7. Team meetings are a great opportunity for you to shift the focus to learning, model fallibility, and curiosity. They also let you ensure an equal distribution of speaking time, foster social sensitivity, and in general support your team in creating a psychologically safe space.

Various meeting types can benefit from a short lessons-learned discussion at the end of the meeting. These conversations can be important at the end of a milestone or goal, in a progress meeting, or even after a team-building workshop.

This conversation can be set up by using three quick questions:

1. What went well?
2. What could have gone better?
3. How do we ensure we do better next time?

* * *

Because strong communication is key to your team's success, you'll reap benefits from setting up an array of communication systems adapted to your needs, those of your team, and the organization. In many cases, we just let tradition or our organization dictate the terms of these systems and end up with systems that don't work for us. Thinking ahead about what formal communication strategies you want to try helps you avoid falling into clichés such as boring meetings or interminable memos. Informal communication strategies, while potentially less visible, can become an important foundation for trust and openness in your team.

Setting up and maintaining good communication within your team is a continuous effort. As things evolve, so must your communication strategies.

Also, no matter how good your communication systems are, chances are that, at some point, conflict will still arise in your team. Conflict can bubble up when teams change structure (i.e., members enter or leave the team and the team cycles back from a performing stage to an earlier forming or storming phase) and in periods of rapid changes or uncertainty in the organization. It can also appear when your communication systems break down, stress levels are high, or individual members are having problems or are burnt out.

Thus, it is also important to have strategies in place to deal with conflict, and we will cover these in Part IV.

PART IV

RESOLVING CONFLICT

CHAPTER 10
UNDERSTANDING CONFLICT

FROM day one, things started to go poorly between Morgan and me. A recent graduate, Morgan thought she was being hired as an independent professional and was never told, until her meeting with me, that she would be part of a team. My team, to be precise. She did not appreciate the idea and made it very clear at every opportunity.

But she was extremely professional, so she did her work, attended meetings, and to the best of her ability, ignored, averted, or limited her team participation. I avoided confronting her about her attitude. I told myself it was because I understood how she was feeling, having been promised things that did not turn out to be true. I also told myself that the problem would go away: she would see that I was just looking to get better results by bringing us all together, and she would get on board. I would pile up work on other people just to give her a wide berth. I wasn't asking the same of her as I was asking from other team members.

Yet, giving her space only strengthened her stance. Eventually, the situation had become so untenable that it erupted in an unplanned, public confrontation in the middle of the open office. I paid a high price for ignoring the conflict.

WHAT IS CONFLICT?

Conflict is a social construct with no universally agreed upon definition. However, based on a review of conflict in organizational settings, Afzalur Rakhim, in his book *Managing Conflict in Organizations*, proposes the following: "an interactive process manifested in incompatibility, disagreement or dissonance within or between social entities (i.e., individuals, groups, organizations, etc)."[54]

I particularly like this definition because of the "within" terminology. If the social entities are individuals, it follows that conflict can also be internal conflict, which is the particular aspect of conflict I will cover in Chapter 10.

Rakhim notes, based on the same review, that conflict definitions have some common elements, including:

- Recognized opposing interests between entities in a *zero-sum* situation.
- A *belief* on each side that the other party will thwart (or is thwarting) their interests.
- It implies *actions* by one or both sides that lead to the thwarting of other's goals.
- Conflict is a *process* developing from relationships and reflecting past interactions.

Let's take a moment to notice some interesting points here. First, the people inside the conflict see only a *zero-sum* scenario. They seem unable to realise the situation might have a win-win alternative.

Second, there is a perception not only of antagonism, but of wilful antagonism, and we believe that the actions taken by the other person are evidence to support this belief.

And lastly, a key aspect: conflict is a *process*. What you are seeing right now is the tip of an iceberg that has long extensions into the murky waters of the past. This concept of conflict as a process is highly useful. It gives us a thought framework for conflict that lets us tackle it more effectively.

A framework for thinking about conflict

In public health, we talk about primary, secondary, and tertiary prevention. Primary prevention is being way ahead of the curve, implementing upstream health strategies that will prevent an accident or disease from happening at all. Think of speed limits to prevent car accidents and limiting consumption of fat to avoid heart disease.

Secondary prevention is about reducing the impact of a disease or accident that has just happened, in many cases by early detection to allow halting or reversing its progress. Airbags in cars are one example, as they limit the damage of an accident. A regular visit to the ob/gyn to allow for early detection of cervical cancer also falls into this category.

Tertiary prevention is about palliating the consequences to quality of life of a disease or accident that has already happened. Lifelong treatments to control diabetes and physical therapy after a car accident would fall into this category.

We can borrow this three-tier framework to think about conflict and how to approach it. When handling conflict, your primary prevention techniques are the strategies we talked about in previous chapters: solid formal and informal communication systems, caring for people as people, developing individual and team relationships, and so on.

When conflict arises, you may find yourself in a situation with low-level, simmering conflict first. If you choose to ignore it, however, it may explode into an ugly confrontation in which egos and trust get damaged.

Secondary prevention for conflict has to do with detecting rising conflict early on and daring to address the elephant in the room before it squashes everybody. Tertiary prevention is about repairing relationships and trust when conflict has escalated, or when an unplanned, uncontained confrontation has taken place, as it happened to me with Morgan. In this chapter we'll tackle secondary and tertiary prevention approaches to conflict.

Styles of conflict-handling

Researchers have identified five different ways in which we respond to conflict[55], depending on where we each stand in two separate dimensions: one related to concern for ourselves and the second one to concern for others. We can see these in the figure below.

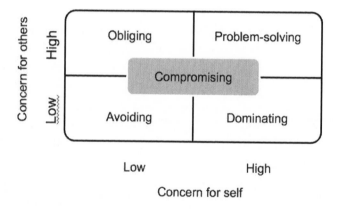

To help explain these conflict-handling styles, let's imagine you have a conflict with one of your team members, Paju.

The first response to conflict is **avoiding** it, that is, inaction. You don't do anything at all and hope that the conflict with Paju will go away on its own. Researchers say this stance comes from a low concern for others coupled with a low concern for oneself. My own impression is that our culture and upbringing have a lot to do with it as well. If we come from a society where conflict is frowned upon, we may become over the years excellent at this strategy, almost unconsciously withdrawing from a confrontation.

The second response is **obliging** or accommodating, where you would basically neglect your own needs or wants in order to satisfy Paju's demands or needs. There is selfless generosity in this style, stemming from a higher level of concern for others than for one's own needs.

The third style is **dominating** or competing, where you would disregard Paju's needs in order to satisfy your own. This dominating style can be seen in a competitive person who attempts to win an argument at any cost. It also can be seen in a person who is standing up for his or her rights or defending highly cherished values.

The fourth style is **compromising**, where you would negotiate an intermediate solution, with Paju conceding in some aspects and you in others, either by splitting the difference or exchanging concessions. It involves a give-and-take game and is a middle ground between obliging and dominating.

The fifth style is **problem-solving** or **collaborating**. It stems from a double high concern for others and for yourself. Dominating and obliging are both win-lose scenarios, while compromising and avoiding can be seen as no-win-no-lose scenarios. Problem-solving, on the other hand, is a win-win scenario. Here you would collaborate with Paju in order to find a creative and constructive solution that isn't "borderline acceptable" to both of you, but that actually creates value for both of you.

In real life, we probably mix our conflict-handling styles quite a bit, depending on the other person's stance, how important the matter is, or how much time we have. We may choose to avoid or oblige in a petty misunderstanding or strike a dominating style on an urgent matter while focusing more energy on reaching a compromise or collaboration in more important matters.

In general, however, when it comes to long-term conflict handling with your team some styles work better than others.

Repeated avoidance may lead to an accumulation of tensions, stress, a breakdown in communication and ultimately less productivity in your team. If conflict usually happens at meetings, for example, people will start dreading meetings, or even coming to work, resulting in absenteeism. The quality of teamwork may deteriorate and cliques may form. Avoidance may also lead to a nasty, unplanned, uncontained confrontation from which it will be harder to rebound.

Being obliging or dominating, while satisfying in the short term for one or both of the parties involved, can also pile up resentment and, therefore, tension and stress. Getting the outcome you want through a dominating position can be gratifying, of course. But it rarely solves the underlying issue, so the problem may reappear later on. Obliging gives you the short-term satisfaction of avoiding confrontation, but may decrease your confidence or foster resentment against the person. Ultimately, both obliging and competing positions may lead to decisions out of line with your team's or the organization's interests.

While compromise or collaboration can take more time and energy in the short run, in the long run, by truly solving the problem, you ensure both you and your team come out stronger on the other side.

Observe yourself for a time and note your preferred style for handling conflict. This is a good starting place for shifting our conflict-handling strategies where we consider this necessary.

APPROACHES FOR HANDLING CONFLICT

Here we'll discuss general strategies for effective conflict resolution through compromise or collaboration. When a conflict is brewing in your team, these strategies will come in handy. In Chapter 11, we'll move into strategies to handle specific conflict situations.

Know the drivers of conflict

When you're facing conflict in your team, take a moment to analyse whether it truly stems from differences in opinion, from lack of communication inside the team, or from more subtle drivers affecting one or two people individually.

We're all human beings, and sometimes we let the worst bits of ourselves show in difficult or stressful periods. Personal issues, such as conflicts at home, a divorce or separation, illnesses or deaths in the family can momentarily change how individuals relate to others in the team. Burnout at work can also make people more aggressive, distant, or conflictive.

Even more banal issues can create temporary friction in our teams. Many of us grow impatient and cranky when we've been sleep deprived or under tension for long periods. I, for one, am known to become very impatient if I'm hungry.

Some conflicts may stem from individual issues like lack of confidence, personal antagonism between team members, jealousy, or big egos.

Change is a big driver of conflict. Most people are consciously or subconsciously reluctant or even afraid of change. If a big change is happening in the organization, or on your team, expect conflict.

Figuring out the subtle drivers, if any, in a particular conflict, can give you an edge in finding creative solutions for handling it more effectively.

Tackle conflict sooner rather than later

You can safely assume that conflict will fester if ignored for too long. I've seen tiny insignificant problems grow completely out of proportion because they were not acknowledged and seemingly huge differences melt away once people sat down to talk about them.

Tackle conflict early. Good communication systems allow for robust primary prevention approaches, but not even the best communication system can prevent conflict every time. Conflict will arise, and you'll have to deal with it. Accepting this as just one more item in your job description as a team leader makes it easier to just pull up your sleeves and tackle it proactively.

Approaches to conflict vary from culture to culture. Some cultures are unafraid of conflict and even cherish it. While in others any raising of voices or direct confrontation is highly frowned upon. Those of us coming from a culture that avoids conflict may find stepping up and addressing it harder. Still, as a direct result of learning to avoid conflict, many of us are acutely attuned to rising tensions. Use this sense to your advantage. Only, instead of avoiding it, bring it up to the light.

To tackle conflict early, in secondary prevention mode, we need to become comfortable with speaking out about the tension in the room. Of course, this exposes us to people denying that tension or conflict. We can use general terms such as "issue" or "situation" and avoid those with negative connotations such as "conflict," "problem," or "confrontation," labels which may not feel right to someone. Even if you know for a fact that Jason and Sam threw their laptops at each other in a past meeting, you can still say, "I heard that you and Jason had some issues the other day? Can we talk about that?"

In cultures or work environments where bluntness is appreciated, however, a more direct approach could work just fine and may even be preferable to beating around the bush.

Listen to all sides of the story first

In your proactive approach to resolving conflict, the first step is to identify that conflict exists and decide you're going to address it right away. The second step is to gather information. Usually there are as many stories as participants to a conflict, and in order to get the whole picture, you need to listen to all the stories first.

Depending on your communication style and the culture and work environment you're in, you may want to talk to all participants in the conflict at the same time or instead go around asking each person what they feel is happening.

If you can't, for some reason, collect every side of the story, still keep in mind that there are other sides to it. Also, be aware you may have more affinity for certain members of your team than you have for others. While there's nothing wrong with this, in cases of conflict you need to be aware of any potential biases you may have and openly listen to all sides of the story to be able to act fairly and impartially.

If it's you who has a problem with someone else, listening to the other side of the story is even more important. We'll go through a specific strategy for this in Chapter 11.

Remember people mostly have good intentions

Lars came to see me in a rage. He was upset because Yul hadn't included him among the trainers for the upcoming workshop. He'd been developing the materials for his part in the workshop, but then, yesterday he'd received the program only to find he wasn't on it. When we went to talk to Yul, it turned out that he'd not included Lars among the trainers because he remembered Lars saying that he was too overwhelmed with work that week! He thought he was being considerate to Lars and doing him a favour by not putting him on the program.

Our brains are wired to jump to conclusions based on only the available information (the "what-you-see-is-what-there-is" phenomenon we discussed earlier), filling in the blanks with assumptions. If you can't help but make assumptions, then assume good intentions until you are proven wrong. Most people are inherently nice. We don't wake up each morning with a plan to mess up our colleagues' lives. We want to work, get results, and get credit and praise for our accomplishments.

When tackling a conflict, make sure to make a little mental note about people's general good intentions. This reminder helps prevent accusations and encourages listening with an open mind. This is harder when you yourself are facing a conflict with someone than when you're acting as a mediator, but keeping people's good intentions in mind will lead to a more positive conversation.

Contain it

When addressing conflict head on, it is best to do it in a contained setting. If you work in an open office, spare innocent bystanders from your discussion and the increased tension. Find an office with a closed door for your meeting. Choose a neutral space, neither your office nor the other person's office. Planning your encounter in a contained setting signals you want to discuss something serious and may help get people in the right frame of mind to resolve the situation.

Then ensure you create a contained, *psychologically safe* space. Create non-physical boundaries for the conflict that allow people to feel more comfortable addressing it. You can do this by applying many of the techniques we've seen so far in the book. You can explain why you're here today, what the goal is (e.g., not vent your frustrations but finding workable solutions that are acceptable to all), set rules upfront for the meeting (e.g., no interrupting, no accusations, listening with an open mind, making a request rather than a complaint), and ensure you have a structure for conducting the meeting and that everyone knows it. (We'll see examples in Chapter 11.)

Avoid "ganging up" on people

One thing that quickly raises resistance and defensiveness is when someone feels singled out, believing that everyone else is against him or her. Preventing this feeling and thus the resistance requires paying attention to the obvious and also the subtle things that may generate it.

Among the obvious ways, do your homework and listen to all sides of the story first, as then you'll be better positioned for maintaining an impartial stance. If things are highly polarized, you may want to state your impartiality upfront.

Also, realize that people can *perceive* you're ganging up on them through insidious little things. If you're the mediator in a conflict, try to get into the room last to avoid people believing you've already been talking to one party or the other. Watch how you seat everyone around a table. Avoid having several people on one side and one sole person on the other or people sitting down on opposite sides according to the clique they belong to. If because of the seating arrangements someone has to be singled out, make sure that person is you.

Let people save face

When I was about to complete my graduate studies, my relations with my advisor had reached an all-time low. Rumours had reached me that he intended not to attend my dissertation, which was unheard of and against the university's terms. I discussed with a mentor how best to broach the subject with my advisor, proposing to just show him the university's rules and let him know he couldn't get away with not coming.

My mentor stopped me short. "Do you want to prove him wrong or do you want him to come to your dissertation willingly? If you do that, he might come, but it'll be grudgingly, and that won't really help solve your conflict with him."

As much as I wanted to get back at my advisor and show him he was wrong, my mentor had a point. I could choose the short-term satisfaction of being right, or try to build a more productive relation in the future by finding a way for him to come willingly to my dissertation.

As satisfying as proving you were right or venting some of your frustration over a conflict can be, chances are this will lead to resentment, not to conflict resolution. In this situation, it helps to ask yourself, "Do I want to be right or do I want to solve the conflict?"

If it is the latter, then follow Dale Carnegie's timeless advice and make sure you give the other person a way to save face.[56] Just as you hate being proven wrong, or caught in a mistake, so does the other person. Allowing people to save face subtracts nothing from you and may make solving the problem constructively and for the long term easier.

In the end, when I went to talk to my advisor, I told him how important it was for me that he supported me during my dissertation, and I gently reminded him of the date (even though I had shared it with him several times before). He said he'd planned a vacation on those dates. I bit back my impulse to show him the university rules and waited quietly. He started talking to himself about how he could rearrange his vacation to be present for my dissertation. The day of my dissertation he not only showed up but he also gave a very nice speech about me.

* * *

Having strong communication systems provides you with a great primary prevention approach to conflict. But chances are, no matter how good your communication strategies may be, conflict will appear at one point or another.

As we've discussed, approaches to conflict include avoiding it, obliging or dominating the other person, or compromising and problem-solving. Among these, compromise and problem solving are better options for truly resolving the conflict, as they focus on a win-win outcome.

When conflict happens, make sure you're prepared for it and capable of detecting it early. Here's where your secondary or even tertiary prevention approaches to conflict come in. Be proactive and do something about it as soon as you realize conflict is there.

In this chapter, we've discussed general strategies to use when handling conflict. In the next chapter, we will discuss tools that you can use in specific conflict situations, whether you are helping a team member who is having internal conflict, mediating a conflict between two or more of your team members, or resolving an issue between you and someone else.

CHAPTER 11
STRATEGIES FOR RESOLVING CONFLICT

NISA came into my office and closed the door. She seemed very agitated and told me she wanted to cancel her attendance to the upcoming international meeting where she was to present her work. I asked her why and listened attentively. She started off by telling me she had no time and was overwhelmed. The deadline was upon us, and she wouldn't be able to hand in a quality paper in time. She also thought the results we were going to present weren't strong enough for the high level of the meeting.

I didn't agree or disagree but asked some open-ended questions instead. "If we decide to go along with this meeting, what kind of support would you need in order to make the deadline? What makes you think the results aren't strong enough to be presented?"

In this way we finally got to the root of the problem--she didn't think she could do it. She thought she was too junior to go as our representative, and she was paralysed with the idea of having to speak to a full auditorium in a language that wasn't her native tongue.

It wasn't that the first issues she had cited were untrue. She did believe the deadline was too tight and the results not strong enough. But at some level she also knew these were issues she could solve because she had done similar things countless times before. These excuses were her rationalizing whatever fears she was feeling underneath.

PERSONAL CONFLICT

As we have seen from the definition of conflict, conflict isn't always external--it can be internal. Here, one of your team members is going through a difficult period; the conflict is intrapersonal. Bear in mind, many times what we perceive as external conflict may originate mostly from internal conflict.

Just as you can be a mediator or facilitator when people are having *interpersonal* conflict with other team members, so also you can be a mediator or facilitator when one of your team members is having *intrapersonal* conflict.

You may think addressing individual conflict is not your role as a team leader, and if your team members are having internal issues, they can go talk them out with friends or a professional. This might well be the case. But, in some instances, such as in Nisa's example, intrapersonal conflict may have to do with professional issues such as lack of confidence in one's work, demotivation, or burnout.

Even when the issues your team member is going through are of a personal matter, the consequences may still spill over into the person's professional sphere. Supporting your team members through a hard time can also be key in gaining their trust. It may get them back on their feet with their heads in the project sooner. Therefore, supporting them personally, may in the medium term benefit you and the whole team.

Moreover, as we have seen, a key characteristic of a good team leader is caring about people as people. So, within certain limits and boundaries, your support as a mediator of internal conflict can be important.

You can assist your team member by proactively creating a contained setting to deal with this conflict. By providing a safe space to talk and open up, you're tackling an issue that further down the road may affect their performance or turn into interpersonal conflict.

In many scenarios, all people need is someone to provide active listening and caring in this safe setting, in order to come to terms with his or her issue. If more assistance is needed, you can provide advice and mentoring, or suggest referrals (e.g., to HR, to professional help, to training or coaching) when helping is beyond the scope of your abilities or mandate.

Common issues you may have to deal with are someone feeling overwhelmed or burnt out, or lacking confidence. You may encounter personal issues such as death or illness in the family and separation or divorce. There are a number of simple tools you can use to support your team member in this setting.

"Rubber-ducking"

Among programmers, the term "rubber-ducking" is used to ask someone to hear you out while you talk about your issue out loud--but not necessarily to provide advice. The term is sometimes attributed to a story in the book, *The Pragmatic Programmer*, by Andrew Hunt and David Thomas, where a programmer worked through debugging his code by explaining it out loud line-by-line to a rubber duck.[57]

Most of us have felt the positive impact of the "rubber duck effect" at some point. When trying to explain something to someone else--or to an inanimate object--we suddenly stumble into what the problem is and what a solution might look like. The effect has been attributed to a slower, more deliberate and detailed describing of the problem when we are talking to someone else--or writing--than when we're just thinking it through.

It also helps when the other person knows little or nothing about the issue, forcing us to review or describe assumptions that we've taken for granted. Finally, when the other person (or the rubber duck) listens without interrupting, we're able to unravel our train of thought without distraction.

So as a leader, many times your job is just to provide a warm, human-sized rubber duck for your team. The advantage is you're more empathetic than a rubber duck. The disadvantage is that we humans have a harder time listening without interrupting.

If required, once you're done dutifully listening, you can ask some open-ended questions to help the person think things through or uncover wrong or unhelpful assumptions. Just providing active listening and insightful questioning can solve a large percentage of your team members' issues. You don't need to do any more than that.

Normalizing

If you've ever been to a medical lab for a blood test and, before inserting the needle into you, the nurse told you, "Some people may feel a small sting," then you've been on the receiving end of a normalizing effort.

Normalization is a tool used regularly by counsellors, therapists, teachers, and health personnel, and we can all use it when listening to someone else's problems or feelings. As stated in *Interviewing and Brief Therapy Strategies*, "normalization attempts to reframe client problem situations as being understood as human."[58] It aims to reassure the person that what they're thinking or feeling is normal under the circumstances, and it can implicitly show empathy for the person's current situation.

For example, when Pat came to tell me he wasn't able to negotiate an agreement with the juridical department, he was upset about the stalemate, and he was also upset because he hadn't succeeded at such a "simple" task. When I told him it had taken me six months to reach any sort of agreement with them the last time, his second worry disappeared and Pat could better focus on a strategy to get out of the stalemate.

Phrases such as "I can see why you're angry. I would be angry too under such circumstances" or "A lot of people are having trouble with the new software," can go a long way toward reassuring a person and refocusing them on solutions, as their feeling of being "the only one with this problem" disappears.

Creating a problem-solving springboard

If after listening and normalizing the person is yet unable to find a solution to their problem, you can help them build a problem-solving springboard. Ask the person to enlist the skills she possesses that are important in solving this issue and to give you specific examples of when she has done something even remotely similar in the past.

In the case of Nisa, we first made a list of the times she had successfully spoken in front of a big audience, then we made a list of the times she had successfully maintained conversations in her second language. Finally, I reminded her of a number of times she had very successfully represented our organization. Thus, while we had no previous examples of her representing the organization in front of a big audience while speaking in a second language, we did have a good number of examples of all these three items separately. It then became evident that the stretch for her was putting these three together, but framing it from the angle of adding up previous achievements helped her see it as a reachable goal.

From there, it was easier for her to come up with a plan of action to be ready for this presentation. I asked what outside support she would need. She requested support with rehearsing her presentation and asked for a contact person at the meeting.

Once we've dug down to the core issues, we can create a

problem-solving framework and guide our team member through it. The idea is not to provide the solutions but to accompany the person as she or he finds these solutions by themselves and make sure we provide any additional external support needed.

A guiding question you can use to help your team members find their own solutions is "What would you recommend to a colleague with a similar problem?"

Personal issues

Your team and staff are human beings, not robots. And whatever is affecting them in their personal lives will, in many cases, have an impact on their work. Some people are better than others at separating professional and personal life and are able to leave their personal issues at the office door, to a certain extent. The majority, however, are not as good at this. So chances are that you'll find, on more than one occasion, your once super-efficient team member now handing in sloppy work, missing deadlines, calling in sick, or arriving late too many times, or acting apathetic, un-participative, aggressive, impatient or on edge.

As for anything else, if you have established a trust system, asking them what is going on and lending a sympathetic ear can go a long way. You can't help them solve their personal problems, but most of us can do at least three things to provide support to a team member facing hard personal situations:

Reassurance. In many cases, your team member knows he is doing poorly at work and this is adding to his angst over their personal issues. Having you, as a team leader, know and understand that he is going through some personal issues may provide some relief. Remind this person that he's a great team member and reassure him you know this is something temporal and he'll bounce back in due time.

Unburdening. Brainstorm ways the person can have some

more time to dedicate to personal issues. In most cases, we can always provide some space or support at work that will take off some of the professional burdens for a while so he or she can concentrate on the personal ones until the worst part is over. In some cases, you can even provide some paid or unpaid leave.

Be creative. Think in terms of the type of support you'd like from your team if you were in a similar situation. You can bring other team members on board. If you've managed to form a solid, cohesive team, people will be happy to help out their colleague in distress.

Ensuring a plan is in place to alleviate most negative consequences of the team member's distraction can go a long way to both reassure him or her and also ensure the team's work is covered in all situations.

Reminders of professional help available. While resistance to mental health support is slowly decreasing, many people still dislike hearing they might need "help." The truth is, many of us will go through an episode of depression or anxiety or other mental health issue at least once in our lives. This means that never requiring professional help is actually the atypical situation, not the other way around.

If you've built enough trust with your team member, be sure to remind them that professional help is available (from HR to medical, mental health, counselling, and training). If appropriate, remind him or her of the plans and options covered by the organization. We can't decide what type of professional help our team member requires, but supporting them and orienting them is something we can definitely do.

Know your limits

You're a team leader, and it's important to remain within the limits of that position. You can coach and support, and you should do so for professional issues. You can provide access to training, and you can always lend a sympathetic ear to personal and professional issues. But health issues, including mental health issues and other personal issues are outside our areas of competence.

For our own good and that of our team members who we are trying to help, recognizing our limits is crucial. In these scenarios, our role is limited to reminding people that professional help is available or referring them to HR or other appropriate resources.

We must also remember to take care of ourselves and having to deal with issues outside what we're required or equipped for can be a source of stress and anxiety. Know your limits and kindly but firmly enforce those boundaries with your team.

CONFLICT BETWEEN TWO OR MORE TEAM MEMBERS

The other type of conflict you'll face is interpersonal conflict, which can include you and a team member or two or more team members, where your role would be more a mediating one. In either case, the same general principles apply: tackle it sooner rather than later, call for a meeting in a contained space, and prepare yourself beforehand.

Let's start by looking at conflict between two team members where you would act as a mediator.

The situation had gotten so out of hand that Gina and Pat, two of my team members were almost not speaking to each other anymore. When I asked Gina why the report wasn't done yet, she said it was because Pat hadn't completed the last of the analyses. When I asked Pat why the data analysis was late, he told me it was because Gina had not yet filled in part of the data forms. I knew both of them to be very responsible, proactive professionals, so all this naming and blaming wasn't a good sign. Eventually, they both came to talk to me, independently, requesting support because the situation had become very tense.

I asked if they would agree to a meeting with me as a mediator. They did. I prepared my toolkit.

Break the ice

I start a tense meeting by requesting that each participant "tell me the one thing you admire the most about your colleague."

This request has three immediate effects: First, people are startled. Most of us approach such meetings from a defensive position, feeling angry with the other person, even if we are in theory agreeing to a meeting to solve the situation. This request can break the defensive barrier that people have brought along for the meeting.

The second effect is refocusing. If Pat and Gina were thinking daggers at each other, now they have to think fast to come up with a positive trait. The mental shift from negative to positive helps redirect the meeting into a more collaborative frame.

The last effect is what I like to call "melting." We all like receiving compliments. Having the person you're so angry at say something they deeply admire about you will, no matter how hard we try to avoid it, melt away part of our anger.

Pat said that he most admired Gina's engagement to the work in the clinic while Gina said she admired Pat's willingness to step in and help other team members. The ambience in the room warmed noticeably.

Then I explained the methodology we were going to use in the meeting, a technique commonly known as "giraffe language."

Giraffe language

Giraffe language, or "non-violent communication," is the best approach I've found so far for successfully solving conflict between individuals, whether at work or in a personal setting. It is credited to the American clinical psychologist Dr Marshall

Rosenberg, who founded the Center for Non-Violent Communication, an organization that continues to teach and spread Dr. Rosenberg's legacy. Non-violent communication got the nickname "Giraffe language", after the animal symbols developed by Dr Rosenberg to explain the approach.[59]

The giraffe is the first of these animals. As the story goes, it was chosen as a symbol of non-violent or compassionate communication because, supposedly, it is the land animal with the biggest heart, since it has to pump up blood all the way up to the giraffe's brain through that long neck. (In truth, the title of biggest heart for a land animal is held by the African elephant.)

The second animal is the jackal, representing competitive communication, a type of communication based on judging, accusing, and criticising. For example, in jackal language, we would say: "You're so lazy that I always end up doing all the work." In giraffe language, the phrase would translate to "I think we're not dividing tasks equally."

Giraffe language, particularly in its original form, may seem like a very "soft" approach for certain working environments, particularly for organizational cultures with higher levels of competition or aggressiveness, strongly hierarchical, or with an ethos of ignoring conflict. It can also be challenging in cultures where it is not appropriate to acknowledge or talk directly about a conflict. Whether you decide that giraffe language is appropriate for your own culture and organization or not, there are still many individual elements from it that you can apply to your conflict situation or tweak to fit your organization's culture. Many of the underlying principles used in giraffe language apply to other conflict-resolution techniques as well.

A meeting based on the giraffe language methodology has four simple steps and a series of common sense recommendations or rules that are agreed upon by all parties at the beginning of the meeting. Your roles as a mediator are to explain the methodology, guide people through the four steps, and gently remind people of the rules as the meeting progresses.

The rules are:

- To listen actively and avoid interrupting.
- To avoid using generalisation words such as "always/never," "everybody/nobody."
- To avoid using value judgements "good/bad," "normal/not normal" "correct/incorrect," "should/ought/must," and of course adjectives such as "lazy" "arrogant," "rude."
- To accept responsibility for one's feelings or reactions.
- Complaints and assumptions are not allowed.
- Give specific examples, not generalities.
- Agree to disagree.

Once the rules have been set out and everybody has agreed on them, you can start into the four steps. Each person will go through the four steps sequentially, and then it will be the other person's turn.

Step 1. Describe the situation. The first step is asking the first person to describe the situation without judgement, using merely facts. This is needed because most of us usually make observations containing explicit or implicit judgements, such as "You were so rude when you interrupted in the meeting" or "You should be more careful when you're presenting." Judgements and criticism trigger defensiveness in the other person, which then blocks or complicates any further conflict resolution. Instead, people are requested to tell what happened in a neutral way and to provide specific examples, in order to avoid generalisations.

Without this framework, Pat might say, "She's been ignoring me every time I ask her to fill out the forms!" Within this framework such a statement is not accepted. ("Ignoring" is an assumption. "Every time" is a generalization.) In giraffe language, the descriptive statement would be something like "I sent Gina two emails asking for the forms last week. On Monday, I went to ask her in person, but she was on the phone and didn't answer me and later didn't come to find me." Those are the *facts*: specific, devoid of assumptions and interpretations.

Step 2. Explain your reaction. In the original giraffe language, the second step is "Express your feelings." Now, talking about feelings is uncommon in work environments. But the truth is that if Gina's behaviour hadn't triggered a negative feeling in Pat, there would be no conflict. Thus, it's helpful to identify what feelings the described scenario triggered in the recipient.

If you don't feel comfortable using the term "feelings," you can ask the person to simply explain what their reaction was to the situation he or she just described. Pat could say, for instance, "This annoyed me as I was already feeling overwhelmed with all the work."

The second step usually brings up phrases with the format "When you do X, I react in Z way." Here it's important to remind the participants that, as stated in the rules, each of us is responsible for our own feelings or reactions.

Giraffe language, like many other conflict-resolution techniques, shifts the focus from "You" (e.g., "You did," "You said") to "I" (e.g., "I reacted," "I felt," "I think").

This allows for two things. First, for Pat to recognize he could've reacted in a different way, perhaps by shrugging it off or recognizing that he came at a bad time and just coming back later. The second is to allow Gina a peek into what her actions or inactions triggered for Pat, without any blame or accusation, and thus facilitating empathy.

Step 3. Identify the need. The third step is to identify what need is going unfulfilled and is triggering the negative reaction. Human needs, including in the workspace, comprise understanding, support, recognition, autonomy, affection, safety (psychological safety), and so on.

For example, Pat could say, "I need your help to complete these forms so we can conclude the report" or "I would like you to understand how it complicates my task when forms are filled out incorrectly" or "I need you to recognize that I am overwhelmed as well, but we still need to complete this report."

Phrases in step three read like:

- "My need is X"
- "...because I want/would like/need X"
- "I need/I would want."

Step 4. Make a request. Finally, this process leads naturally to step four, where the person makes a request that would help him or her fulfil the identified need. A request is different from a complaint. Complaints are not allowed in giraffe talk. A request has no judgment or criticism and is phrased as a question, implying that we will accept "no" as an answer. Specific requests normally work better than general ones.

Step four has phrases that take the format:

- Please, would you...?
- I would appreciate it if you could...
- Are you willing to...?
- Would you agree to...?
- Could I ask you to...?

To conclude his intervention, Pat could say, for instance, "I would appreciate it if we could sit together for two hours this week to finalize the forms and the report, and you could give me your undivided attention."

The response. After person A completes the four steps, it's time for person B to talk. However, instead of letting person B go straight into the four steps of giraffe language, I find it useful to give a space for person B to respond to person A first.

This response is *also* formulated in giraffe language. The response includes:

- Mirroring of what the person just said, in order to ensure a correct understanding.
- An acknowledgement of the other person's feelings and needs (or an apology, if adequate).
- An acknowledgement of the request, with any clarifications if needed.

For example, Gina's answer could be "I hear that you're upset because you're overwhelmed, and you'd like us to work together on this. I'm sorry I didn't get back to you on this in time. I think your suggestion is a good idea. We can definitely take two hours this week to work on it."

If person B feels unwilling or unable to address person A's request at this time, it is better to say that he or she will at least consider it. For example, Gina could say, "I'm overwhelmed too, but I understand the importance of completing the forms this week. Can I get back to you on your request, so I have time to think how to best address it?"

Now that person B has proven he or she was paying attention, and has, if appropriate, answered the request, it's person B's turn to go through the four steps and person A's turn to listen actively.

When person B finishes, person A responds in a similar fashion, mirroring back to make sure he or she understood and has been listening actively, recognizing the other person's feelings and needs, and answering the request.

Wrap up. To close the session, as a mediator you can briefly summarize each party's commitments and ask them for corroboration. Ask if they'd like to say anything else and if they believe the meeting was useful. Make sure they agree on a date to follow up on this meeting on their own. For example, I could say to Gina and Pat, "OK, so to summarize, you both agree to meet for two hours this week to complete the forms and report. And moving forward you have agreed to find a more efficient mechanism to fill out these data forms. Is this correct? Am I missing anything?"

In Clinic 19 in the Workbook, you'll find a cheat sheet outlining this mediator process, which you can print out and have at hand whenever you need it.

CONFLICT BETWEEN YOU AND A COLLEAGUE OR TEAM MEMBER

The giraffe language system can be tweaked to serve as a tool when the conflict is between you and someone else. Alexander Kjerulf, author of *Happy Hour is 9 to 5*, proposes a modified version of the giraffe technique, which works beautifully in work scenarios.[60] Over the years, I've tested and tweaked his approach to better adapt it to my own scenarios and needs. Below I'll walk you through this modified approach.

If you have a conflict with a colleague or team member at work, you may not want to explicitly lay out the giraffe technique and its rules, but you can still drive the conversation in a positive direction by using it yourself. Giraffe language prevents conversations from degenerating into mutual accusations and focuses on listening and problem-solving.

At the beginning of Chapter 10, I introduced a conflict I had with my team member Morgan. Morgan did not want to work as part of a team and, hoping to avoid a confrontation, I requested little from her in terms of team-work, until the situation became untenable that we ended up having an angry outburst in the middle of the office. I will use that conflict as an example to discuss my modified approach to solving conflict between you and a team member.

When I calmed down after our very public clash with Morgan, I knew we needed to settle our differences in a more contained, constructive way. Going back to our conflict prevention framework, this was clearly tertiary prevention, or damage control, so I was acting too late, but I still sorely needed to repair my communication with Morgan.

Issue an invitation . The next day I crossed her in the hallway, said, "Hi," politely, and told her, "I think yesterday things got a bit out of hand. We weren't in the best setting for a productive discussion. Do you have half an hour after lunch so we can meet in private in the conference room and discuss things more calmly?"

When issuing this invitation, be specific about when and where you'd like to meet. Make sure the meeting takes place in a private, neutral environment.

Inviting the other person to sit down and speak with you is usually the hardest part of the conflict, mostly because the ego gets in the way. You're acknowledging that a situation has turned sour, so you're the first one to put your cards on the table. The other person always has the option of negating the situation. But, taking this first step shows exactly the kind of leadership and responsibility you're aiming for, and it's in line with our preventive, proactive approach to conflict resolution.

Prepare for the meeting. As usual, prepare your meeting beforehand. Use your regular meeting cheat sheet to decide pre-emptively:

a.   What would be your ideal outcome for the meeting?

b.   How do you want to feel during and after the meeting?

c. Which specific examples you will use for each of the steps in the approach we'll describe below?

If the conflict is too grim or the stakes too high, you may want to role-play your meeting in advance to better prepare for it. Role-playing is widely used to train people to navigate difficult conversations, and many leaders, mediators, and negotiators regularly practice tough meetings in advance if the stakes are too important. Ask a trusted person to help you prepare for the meeting. Explain the situation and let him or her play out the role of the other person. Ask her or him to play it tougher than how you hope the meeting will turn out, so you can be over-prepared.

Step 1. Describe the situation. Once you're at the meeting, start by thanking your team member or colleague for agreeing to meet with you. Then lay out your most objective and neutral view of the situation. Be specific and use examples. Focus more heavily on what *you are doing* than on what the other person is doing. Also, try framing the situation not as "me against you" but as "us against the problem."

Ask the other person if he or she agrees with this description. Give them the opportunity to add anything they think is missing from it. Apply all giraffe rules to your language--no assumptions, judgements, accusations, or generalizations allowed.

For example, when Morgan accepted my request for a meeting, I started it out by saying, "Thanks for accepting to meet today. I think our interaction yesterday got a little bit out of hand. My feeling is we were both tense about the deadline. I noticed I didn't stop to listen to the reasons you don't want to include Tim in the project report. Also, I've noticed at past meetings these previous months we've often been at odds with each other and had a hard time agreeing on teamwork matters. Would you say this is an accurate description of the situation? Am I missing any key points?"

Of course, deep down what I *wanted* to say was "Why are you so adamant about working by yourself and not as a team?!" But I doubt that would've got us far, so I stuck to giraffe language.

Step 2. Acknowledge your part in the conflict. Any time you're using a secondary or tertiary approach to conflict friction has already happened. Because of this, apologising, or at a minimum, acknowledging your part in the conflict is strongly recommended. Note that you don't need to apologise for everything, just for *your part in it*. Only very, very rarely is a single person at fault in a conflict. In most situations, both parties have some stake in creating and maintaining it. Recognize your part. This step helps pave the way for a productive conversation, and in repairing the trust and communication links that were torn down. If this point is particularly hard, remind yourself that your goal is to solve the issue, not to be right.

After Morgan agreed with my description and added that in her opinion our relationship had been somewhat fraught from the beginning, I went on to step two. I told her, "I'm sorry about my reaction yesterday. It was unprofessional and out of line."

Notice I'm not apologising for the whole of our very fraught relationship, but only for this specific issue where I truly believe I could've done better. The apology needs to be sincere, so make sure you're convinced about what you're apologising for.

If you don't want to apologise, you can simply acknowledge your part. For example, I could have said to Morgan, "I was tense yesterday and I reacted in a way that was not constructive."

An important point here is not to expect an apology or acknowledgement in return. If the other person takes your lead and apologises as well, that's great. If not, just continue the conversation. Some people may not apologise in turn, but simply recognise your apology or acknowledgement by saying something like "Thanks for saying that," or "I appreciate you noticing that."

Morgan, having had time to cool off herself, kindly answered my apology with one of her own. "Yeah, I'm sorry too. It was really bad timing for that conversation."

Step 3. Praise the other person. Similar to your conflict-mediating role, when you asked people to say what they most admired about each other, in this step you'll do it yourself. Let the other person know what you most admire or appreciate in him or her at work. Tell them why it's worth it for you to solve the conflict. Is he a great organizer (despite being too much of a perfectionist)? Tell him so. (The first part only!) Is she extremely reliable under tight deadlines? Tell her so!

This step has two advantages. First, it helps you to clearly refocus on the other person's positive side, not just on the things that irritate you. It helps you clarify to yourself why you're even going through all the trouble of repairing your relationship with this person.

Second, as we discussed earlier, it has a "melting" effect. We all like to receive compliments. Receiving praise from someone who you're in conflict with has an even stronger effect. It goes a long way toward creating a constructive setting for the meeting.

I'd always been very clear why I appreciated Morgan's work, so this part came easily. I said, "I know we don't agree on some important issues, but I want you to know that I appreciate your contribution to the organization. I think you do great work with our beneficiaries. You're always on time, efficient in your work, and striving to do things better. So I really think it's important for us to solve this issue and learn to work better together."

If you can't think of a single positive thing to say or any reason you should resolve the conflict with this person, you may need to consider if:

- You need more time to cool off.
- You might need an external mediator to solve this one.

- You want this person to continue being on your team at all.

Step 4. State the consequences. Here we can state the reaction and outline the outcomes of this conflict. How does it make us feel? What does it trigger in us? What other negative consequences are there beyond the two of us? Outlining the consequences of our conflict highlights why it's important for both parties resolve it.

For example, if you and your colleague always end up attacking each other in meetings, you might have realized that not only you have started disliking and evading meetings, but also other people have started disliking and avoiding them. The meetings may have become unproductive and tense because of your bickering with your colleague.

Ask the other person if he or she agrees with the consequences you've pointed out or wishes to add some more, and listen openly to his or her comments.

I told Morgan, "I think the situation between the two of us is starting to negatively affect the rest of the group because of the tension it creates. I definitely believe that yesterday we made quite a number of people uncomfortable with our discussion. Would you agree?"

Step 5. Make a request. Here's where you ask for your ideal outcome. If you did your homework before coming into the meeting, you know exactly what that is. It's time to bring it up and listen to what the other person's ideal outcome would look like.

Do you want to stop criticising each other in meetings? Be more appreciative of each other? Hold more regular constructive and contained meetings like this one to avoid things getting out of hand in the future? Look for ways in which you can work more independently from each other?

Ensure your request clarifies the big picture and also propose specific, actionable steps that can be applied immediately. In many instances, it can also be helpful to offer something in exchange, based on the insights you have gained from this meeting.

If you managed to reframe the situation as "us against the problem" in the previous steps, now you can brainstorm solutions together by focusing on your common ground. Again, listen actively to the other person and don't dismiss their solutions.

My goal with Morgan was to negotiate an agreement that worked for both of us. I didn't want her out of my team, but I did need her to play as a team member more often. She resented being on my team, but she liked the work she was doing. It seemed plausible that we could find a win-win solution.

I said, "I would like you to work more often as part of the team. If I understand correctly from what we've discussed so far, I think you, on the other hand, would like more independence. I would like us to find a solution that works for both of us. Would you agree to work as a team member on project A and contribute with your knowledge and skills if on project D you work on your own?

After some tweaking and negotiating, we did find a working agreement. We also agreed to disagree on the core issue of how the team had been structured, as it seemed clear we couldn't see eye to eye on that point. Most importantly, though, we regained respect for each other, we smoothed over our differences, and we were able to go back to the office and act professionally and even amicably towards each other. We never did become friends, but our relationship greatly improved after that meeting.

Step 6. Close the meeting on a positive note. Whether you've reached an agreement or not, or even if the other person maintained an adamantly negative position, do your best to close the meeting on a positive note. At the very least, the other person agreed to show up and sit down with you to talk. Acknowledge this.

If you've reached an agreement, then summarize it, and choose a date and place to meet to review progress. I even know some people who at this point, if things have worked well during the discussion, decide to ride the wave and go have a beer together!

* * *

Conflict will always happen in our work environments. While many of us have learned to avoid conflict and bury our heads in the sand, actively addressing conflict as soon as it arises can prevent many disagreeable situations and make conflict-resolution encounters easier.

As leaders, we'll not only have to address conflict between ourselves and one of our team members, but we'll also need to be ready to address intrapersonal conflict, usually related to demotivation, lack of confidence, and burnout as well as interpersonal conflicts between two or more members of our teams, where there's a need for a mediator.

Having strategies and tools to address these different conflict scenarios in a systematic way facilitates a proactive approach and can help us to stop fearing conflict and start recognising it as an opportunity for learning and growth.

Epilogue - Under construction

Hopefully, by this point in your reading, you are feeling much more capable and excited about your new leadership role. I hope my own experiences and research have opened new panoramas for you to keep on growing as a leader.

Strong team leaders focus equally on two key aspects, which we've sequentially addressed throughout this book: strategies and mindset. The strategies are the hard, tangible approaches and systems of your work: planning and time management, meeting and team-building tools, formal communication systems, and conflict-resolution approaches.

The mindset aspect has more to do with soft skills, the people side of things. As human beings, our team members have needs and issues that can't be addressed solely through better time management or organizational skills. In many cases, solving the mindset side, and addressing things like motivation, trust, and connection can produce much higher rewards than focusing exclusively on strategies.

Under this aspect, we've discussed things such as maintaining a growth mindset, caring for your people as people, creating group norms that promote psychological safety, maintaining informal communication systems that build trust and cohesion, and building listening and mediator skills to address intrapersonal and interpersonal conflict.

Team leadership is a tough yet highly-rewarding experience. It does get easier the more we practise it, but building a team is always a project under construction. Our team members and we are humans, and as humans, we have our ups and downs.

You may have been working hard to coach and help out the weakest link among your team members, only to realize, just when you feel he's doing much better, that your most solid, reliable team member is having some difficult personal issues and is fast approaching burnout. You can think of this as demotivating and frustrating, or you can rejoice in the continuously changing nature of your work and the new challenges it brings every day.

NEXT STEPS

If you've finished *Build your Dream Team* and are eager for more, visit the website:

www.candela-iglesias.com/resources

On the site, you'll find resources like these:

- **Leadership and Team-building tips.** Read the blog or sign up to the monthly newsletter. Join in the discussion!
- **Build your Dream Team - The Workbook.** Download the printer-friendly companion workbook where you'll find the exercises, templates and cheat sheets mentioned in this book. (PDF format)
- **All eyes on you. Nine steps to creating a memorable presentation.** Leaders need to speak up. Become a better presenter and build your public speaking skills with the strategies, tips and exercises in this booklet. (PDF format)

Acknowledgements

This book would not have happened without the encouragement and guidance of a number of people. I will start by thanking Mark, my writing buddy. It was sheer good luck to find such a great accountability partner. Our weekly meetings and his staunch support helped me navigate this process all the way to publishing!

Thank you to my editor, Miranda Regan, who was patient and professional, helping me create a polished version of this book.

The SPS author community is nothing short of extraordinary. Their cheerfulness, vulnerability, encouragement and selfless time spent on sharing lessons learned has been invaluable. A special thank you to all the amazing people on my launch team for taking time out of their busy schedules to pre-read my book.

I began developing many of the ideas discussed in this book while working as a team leader. I am indebted to the amazing people I've been lucky to have on my teams over the years. I've learned so much from you. I'm also grateful to my amazing colleagues at CIENI who have taught me so much. And to the excellent bosses I've been lucky to have over the years. Thank you to Victor who taught me by example how to create a cohesive team. And of course, to Gustavo, for being a bigger-than-life example of compassionate leadership.

I am, as always, thankful to my amazing family. To my sisters, for never doubting me, for always being there for me and cheering me through this process. Thanks to Mom and Dad for their interest in and excitement about reading all my writings-- even the boring academic ones--throughout the years.

Finally, the biggest thank you of all goes to Gard, for being my solid anchor through this rocky process. Because the first time I told you about my idea of writing a book, you thought it was brilliant, and you proceeded to enumerate for me all the reasons you were convinced I could do it. Because you celebrated every milestone with me and kept reminding me that you were looking forward to reading this book.

NOTES AND REFERENCES

[1] ...let me share with you a forest metaphor I first read in Stephen Covey's long-time bestseller The Seven Habits of Highly Effective People. In his book, Covey tells the forest story a bit differently. When he comes to describing the leader, he says, "The leader is the one who climbs the tallest tree, surveys the entire situation, and yells "Wrong jungle!" Stephen R. Covey, The 7 Habits of Highly Effective People, (UK: Simon & Schuster, 2013).

[2] Margie Warrell is an Australian bestselling author, speaker, commentator and women's advocate. This quote comes from a column she wrote for Forbes on the occasion of Women's Day in 2014. You can read her blog posts and her work in her webpage: www.margiewarrell.com. Margie Warrell, "Dare Bravely, Speak Boldly: 10 Lessons From Leading Women On Closing The Gender Gap," Forbes (6 March 2014).

[3] *John French and Bertrand Raven, back in 1959, researched the sources of power that leaders use to influence others...* Discussions on French and Raven's classic research on sources of power can be found in most textbooks on leadership and organizational behaviour. J.R.P and Raven, B.H., "The Bases of Social

Power," in D. Cartwright (ed.), Studies in Social Power. (Ann Arbor, MI: University of Michigan Press, 1958), 150-67.

[4] *Yet the world abounds with examples of introverts who are great leaders.* Susan Cain, *Quiet: The Power of Introverts in A World that Can't Stop Talking,* (New York: Random House, 2013). You can also see her powerful TED talk on the subject.

[5] *...employees and organizations thrive when intrinsic motivation, not a "carrot and stick" punishment and reward system, is the driving force.* Daniel H. Pink, *Drive: The Surprising Truth About What Motivates Us,* (New York: Penguin Group, 2009).

[6] Two good sources of information about Malala Yousafzai are the Malala Fund website (www.malala.org) and the Nobel Prize's official website (www.nobelprize.org), which has biographies on all its award recipients.

[7] Information on Mark Zuckerberg and Facebook is widely available on the internet. The data here come from Forbes and Investopedia.

[8] *I wrote this book with the support of a superb writing and publishing program created by a twenty-something.* Chandler Bolt is the founder and CEO of the Self-Publishing School, an online programme and community of writers which to date has over 100,000 "students." You can find more about the program at self-publishingschool.com

[9] *...a number of studies suggest that women rate as effective as men as leaders in general...* Here's a meta-analysis of ninty-nine independent samples from ninety-five studies, providing a nuanced review of the issue. Samantha C. Paustian-Underdahl, Lisa Slattery Walker, David J. Woehr, "Gender and Perceptions of Leadership Effectiveness: A Meta-Analysis of Contextual Moderators," *Journal of Applied Psychology* 99(6) (Nov. 2014): 1129-1145.

Zenger-Folkman, a leadership research, assessment and development firm, has collated and analysed data from 450,000 feedback instruments on over 45,000 leaders. Jack Zenger and Joseph Folkman, "Are Women Better Leaders than Men?," *Harvard Business Review* (March 15, 2012).

[10] *If you're a women struggling with these issues...*Two of my favourite books on the subject of women and leadership are:

Lois. P. Frankel, PhD, *See Jane Lead: 99 Ways for Women to Take Charge at Work*. (New York: Hachette, 2007).

Dr Frankel's book is a great resource in particular for new women leaders who are struggling with self-confidence issues. Its premise is that many women are already leading and showing key leadership traits. They're just not identifying themselves as leaders. It's packed with practical advice, examples, and exercises.

Sheryl Sandberg, *Lean In: Women, Work and the Will to Lead* (New York: Random House, 2013).

Sandberg, COO of Facebook and one of the most powerful women in business, brings together research and personal experience in her book. While recognizing the issues that organizations and societies need to tackle to increase women in leadership positions, she focuses on what each woman can do, how to stop unintentionally holding herself back, how to "sit at the table," seek more challenges, and take more risks. You can also watch her 2010 TED talk, "Why We Have Too Few Women Leaders," from which her book was derived.

[11] Carol S. Dweck, PhD, *Mindset: The New Psychology of Success*, (New York: Random House, 2008).

[12] I have collated this list from multiple sources and, as it grew, I added related skills that seemed important to me. One starting point was Andrzej A. Huczynski, David A. Buchanan, *Organizational Behaviour* (Harlow, UK: Pearson Education, 2013).

[13] This quote comes from an article by Fred Kofman, vice-president of leadership and organizational development at LinkedIn and author of *Conscious Business*. Fred Kofman, "Be a Hero: Five Steps to Vanquish Any Problem, LinkedIn Pulse (March 28, 2013).

Among Kofman's many great posts, his two-piece video series on our values and the assumptions we make about people's behaviours is definitely worth a look: "What do you really value?" LinkedIn Pulse. (August 10, 2015)

[14] *Stephen Covey talks about "response-ability"--the ability to choose our own response.* Covey, *2013*.

[15] This quote is widely attributed to Theodore Roosevelt on the internet, but I haven't found a reliable source to prove this. Wikiquotes has a discussion as to its origin in https://en.wikiquote.org/wiki/Talk:Theodore_Roosevelt.

Reliable quotation sites such as Bartlett's quotations don't include this quote among Theodore Roosevelt's sayings. Also, I have not found an original source (book, letter, speech) for the quote.

[16] *Saturation is a concept used in social science research...* See Michael Bloor, Fiona Wood, *Keywords in Qualitative Methods: A Vocabulary of Research Concepts* (SAGE: 2006)

[17] *There are many decision-making processes...* See Chapter 11. Decision Making, in Mason Carpenter, Talya Bauer, Berrin Erdogan, *Principles of Management.* (NP: Flat World Education, 2016). This book is freely available online.

The website Mindtools also has a good overview of decision-making models.

[18] *...a common human bias which authors Dan and Chip Heath, in their New York Times bestseller book Decisions, refer to as the "spotlight effect.* Dan and Chip Heath, *Decisive* (New York: Random House, 2013).

The Heath brothers write about human behaviour and its quirks and how to use this knowledge to obtain better results. Among their three published books, my favourite, and particularly useful if you are interested in achieving change in your organization or your team, is *Switch: How to Change Things When Change Is Hard.*

[19] The Nobel Prize winning psychologist Daniel Kahneman argues that despite the huge amounts of information in the world, we almost always have an opinion or "gut-feeling" about things, even without analysing them, because we put too much weight on the information that is available in front of us, forgetting to weigh in the information we do not possess. A phenomenon he calls "what you see is all there is."

Daniel Kahneman, *Thinking Fast and Slow* (New York: Farrar, Straus, & Giroux, 2011). This book is a long but fascinating read. It draws from the author's long years of research, most of them in collaboration with Amos Tverksy, on how we think and make choices, and the many cognitive biases we fall prey to. Their ground-breaking work contradicted the rational model of decision-making long put forward by economists.

[20] *That paradigm has been changing fast. In his book* Give and Take, *Adam Grant presents research...* Adam Grant, 2013.

[21] *Amy Cuddy, from the Harvard Business School, along with other researchers have shown that projecting warmth (communion or trustworthiness)...* Amy J.C. Cuddy, Mathew Kohut, John Neffinger, "Connect, then Lead," *Harvard Business Review* (Jul-Aug 2013).

[22] Dale Carnegie, *How to Win Friends and Influence People* (London: Random House, 1953).

[23] *Care for your people as people.* I did not find a clear attribution of this quote. Dave Ramsey, author of *The Total Money Makeover*, has used this phrase in a letter to readers called "Dave Says ," appearing in various business sites in 2013. The phrase also appears in: Butch Bellah, *Sales Management for Dummies* (Hoboken, NJ: John Wiley and Sons, 2015), 261.

[24] *Businesses with engaged employees tend to outperform those with disengaged employees ...* Several sources of data point to this, but methodologies and size of data samples vary. Gallup's 2016 Q12 meta-analysis, with 82,000 business/work units and 1.8 million employees is the largest I've found so far. See: James K. Harter, Frank l. Schmidt, Sangeeta Agrawal, Stephanie K. Plowman, Anthony Blue, "The Relationship Between Engagement at Work and Organizational Outcomes." *2016 Q12 Meta-analysis: Ninth Report* (Gallup, April 2016).

[25] *...and one consistent key driver of engagement seems to be the relationship with the immediate supervisor.* Dale Carnegie Training, "What Drives Employee Engagement and Why It Matters" (Dale Carnegie and Associates, 2012).

See also, Dale Carnegie Training, "Enhancing Employee Engagement: The Role of the Immediate Supervisor" (Dale Carnegie and Associates, 2012).

[26] *... it plummets to 2% in employees who are ignored by their managers.* J.

Brandon Rigoni, Ph.D and Bailey Nelson, "The No-Managers Organizational Approach Doesn't Work," *Gallup Business Journal* (5 Feb. 2016).

[27] *...a survey among American workers showed that 54% of employees who believed their managers cared about them personally...* "Enhancing Employee Engagement," 2012.

[28] As you can imagine, nowadays there are many apps and online tools to help you with planning. Among those with free versions, Trello is a simple, easy to use choice, which works better for task management than project management. For more complex projects and larger teams, there's Zoho, writer, Teamwork projects and many others.

[29] *Landmark studies conducted by Henry Mintzberg in the seventies have shown that a manager's activities are "characterized by brevity, variety, and discontinuity."* Henry Mintzberg, "*The Manager's Job. Folklore and Fact,*" Harvard Business Review (Mar.-Apr. 1990).

[30] *...half of the activities they engaged in lasted less than nine minutes...* Henry Mintzberg, *The Nature of Managerial Work* (New York: Harper & Row, 1973).

[31] *In a more recent study of managers, project leaders and others...* Victor M Gonzalez, Gloria Mark, "Constant, Constant, Multi-tasking Craziness: Managing Multiple Working Spheres," Proceedings of ACM CHI (2004).

[32] *Betsy and Warren Talbot, authors and creators of the podcast "An Uncluttered Life" suggest these four rules:* An Uncluttered Life is a website and podcast held by Betsy and Warren Talbot where they share "hacks, workarounds and shortcuts" they have used since 2006 to drop their corporate jobs and sell their possessions to travel the world and proactively create the life of their dreams. Practical, funny and easy-going, it's one of the few websites I follow regularly. These rules are from their podcast and accompanying pdf: Episode 147: 7 Ways to Unclutter your Email.

[33] *It is called the urgent/important matrix, and it is often attributed to D. Eisenhower.* The attribution of this technique to Dwight. D. Eisenhower,

34th President of the United States, seems to be based on a famous quote, "I have two kinds of problems, the urgent and the important. The urgent are not important and the important are never urgent." It is not clear whether the matrix per se is his invention. The quote is from his "Address at the Second Assembly of the World Council of Churches," Evanston, Illinois (August 19, 1954). The speech can be found at the American Presidency Project.

The urgent versus important matrix is in chapter five of Covey, 2013., among other authors.

[34] *The first one is tracking your time-use. Laura Vanderkam, a time-management expert, who covers this issue extensively in her books and blogs, uses a simple spreadsheet called "168-hours"...* Vanderkam also argues that this time-tracking exercise allows us to let go of our "busyness" mentality, by recognizing that even though we're busy we still have a lot of free time in our days and in our weeks. Time-tracking, by virtue of making us aware of how we choose to use this free time, helps us create healthier time-management habits. Vanderkam has written several books and many articles and posts on the subject. You can find her work at www.lauravanderkam.com.

Laura Vanderkam, *168 Hours: You Have More Time Than You Think* (London: Penguin Group, 2010).

[35] Time-tracking apps. I've tried spread-sheets, used the calendar on my phone, and more recently I've settled for the Toggl app (no affiliation), which has a powerful free option, and some paid options that may be interesting if you want to invoice time spent on a project. Other apps include: Hours (iOS), Everhour (Web) and Timely (Web, iOS).

[36] *And willpower is a finite resource that dwindles over the day as we use it up.* Willpower and willpower depletion are fascinating subjects, and a lot of research has accumulated over the years. A large body of data suggests willpower is indeed "a limited resource," but there is some controversy, as some experiments have shown that mood and beliefs have an impact on whether willpower gets depleted or not. For a good online

discussion based on published research see: "What You Need to Know about Willpower: The Psychological Science of Self-Control.,"*American Psychology Association*" (2012).

I've also immensely enjoyed the book, *Switch*, by the Heath brothers, where willpower, how it gets exhausted, and what to do about it are key themes. See: Dan and Chip Heath, *Switch: How to Change Things When Change Is Hard* (New York: Random House, 2010).

[37] *Christine Kane, founder and CEO of Uplevel You, shares a very good test to help you decide whether it is time to let go of someone.* Christine Kane, "The #1 Warning Sign It's Time to Fire an Employee," *Uplevel You Blog.*

[38] Covey 2013, 182.

[39] *... and yet a group is not necessarily the same as a team.* The differences between a group and a team are discussed in detail in many management and organizational behaviour books. I like in particular Andrzej A. Huczynski & David A. Buchanan's *Organizational Behaviour.*

[40] *Research dating back to the 1960s by Bruce Tuckman has shown that disparate teams...* Bruce Tuckman, "Developmental Sequence in Small Groups," Psychological Bulletin 63 (1965), 384-99.

[41] *They set up a team called the "Project Aristotle" tasked with finding an answer by using Google's...* The New York Times published a great review article on Google's quest to find the characteristics of the best teams. See: Charles Duhigg. "What Google Learned from its Quest to Build the Perfect Team," New York Times Magazine (25 Feb. 2016).

[42] *...in the words of Google analyst Julia Rozovsky...* Julia Rozovsky, "The Five Keys to a Successful Google Team," *The Water Cooler Blog. Re:Work* (17 Nov 2015).

[43] *Psychological safety can be defined in a team setting, as "sense of confidence that the team will not embarrass, reject or punish someone for speaking up."* Amy Edmonson, "Psychological Safety and Learning Behavior in Work Teams," *Administrative Science Quarterly* 44:2 (Jun. 1999), 350-383.

[44] *...in order to foster psychological safety it's important to "frame the work as a learning problem not an execution problem."* The quote is from Amy Edmonson TEDx talk at Harvard Graduate School of Education.

"Building A Psychologically Safe Workplace" (2014). She has also published several books and articles on the topic, which you can find at the Harvard Business School Faculty and Research webpage.

[45] *Ibid.*

[46] *Researchers have shown that having high "average social sensitivity" is also a trait of successful teams.* A.W. Woolley, C.F. Chabris, A. Pentland, N. Hashmi, T.W. Malone, "Evidence for a Collective Intelligence Factor in the Performance of Human Groups," *Science* 330 (2010), 686. This is a fascinating experiment on human behaviour and teams.

[47] *The communication process has been defined as "the transmission of information and the exchange of meaning between at least two people."* Andrzej A Huczynski, David A. Buchanan, 2013.

[48] *The communication process, at its most simple, involves a transmitter, a message, and a receiver... Ibid.*

[49] *...humans can use and read up to 21 different facial expressions, and we potentially read fleeting involuntary micro-expressions as well.* Paul Eckman, *Emotions Revealed* (New York: Henry Holt and Co, 2003), *237.*

[50] *... studies show that graphs or images are remembered much better than written words.* It seems as if the first experiment testing this dates back to 1894, when Kirkpatrick showed that after 72 hours, individuals recalled over 65% of pictures seen but less than 30% of words. A good overview of these an other experiments can be found in Stephen Madigan. Picture Memory. In John C. Yullie (Ed.) *Imagery, Memory and Cognition: Essays in Honor of Allan Paivio* (New York, NY: Psychology Press, 1983).

A newer overview, including a review of situations where picture recognition is neither superior nor even comparable to word recognition can be found in: Joyce M. Oates and Lynne M. Reder. "Memory for Pictures: Sometimes a picture is not worth a single word". In Benjamin, A.S. (Ed.), *Successful Remembering and Successful Forgetting: A Festschrift in Honor of Robert A. Bjork.* (New York: Psychology Press) 447-462.

[51] *Adam Grant, organizational psychologist and author of* Give and Take

argues that the sandwich approach can be counterproductive. Adam Grant, "Stop Serving the Feedback Sandwich," LinkedIn Pulse (13 May 2016).

[52] Quiz apps let you create a questionnaire in advance, have people sign in with their smartphones, and answer multiple choice questions as they are shown on a screen. You can then see how many participants voted for each response. Medical doctors love them as they're great for presenting case-studies in a more interactive way. Facilitators use them at the end of a workshop to reinforce what has been learned. I use the free Kahoot! app (no affiliation), but there are many others, both paid and free.

[53] *... you might want to assign a particular person or pair the role of devil's advocate, to avoid bad-decision making due to group-think.* Groupthink is a phenomenon happening in cohesive groups, where "members' strivings for unanimity override their motivation to appraise realistically the alternative courses of action." Andrzej A Huczynski, David A. Buchanan, 2013.

[54] *Afzalur Rakhim, in his book, "Managing Conflict in Organizations," proposes the following...* M. Afzalur Rahim, *Managing Conflict in Organizations* (New Brunswick, NJ: Transaction Publishers, 2010), 16.

[55] *Researchers have identified five different ways in which we respond to conflict...* This five-category scheme for interpersonal conflict handling was first introduced by Blake and Mouton and further developed by Thomas and Kilmann.

R. R. Blake, J. S. Mouton, *The Managerial Grid* (Houston: Gulf Publishing, 1964). R. H. Kilmann, K. W. Thomas, "A Forced-Choice Measure of Conflict-Handling Behavior: The MODE Instrument," *Educational and Psychological Measurement* 37:2 (1973), 309-325.

[56] *...follow Dale Carnegie's timeless advice and make sure you give the other person a way to save face.* Carnegie, 1953.

[57] *The term is sometimes attributed to a story in the book "The Pragmatic Programmer"...* Andrew Hun, David Thomas, *The Pragmatic Programmer: From Journeyman to Master* (NP: Addison Wesley, NP), 95, footnote.

[58] *As used in Interviewing and Brief Therapy Strategies, "normalization*

attempts to reframe client problem situations as being understood as human." Georges Carpetto, *Interviewing and Brief Therapy Strategies: An Integrative Approach* (NP: Ally & Bacon/Longman, 2008), 249.

[59] *This approach has gotten its nickname "Giraffe language"...* You can learn more about Dr Rosenberg, his animal symbols and giraffe language in general at The Center for Non-Violent Communication, www.cnvc.org, which he founded.

[60] *Alexander Kjerulf, author of* Happy Hour is 9 to 5, *proposes a modified version of the giraffe technique which works beautifully in work scenarios.* Alexander Kjerulf, "5 Essential Steps to Resolve a Conflict at Work," The Chief Happiness Officer Blog (31 July 2006). Kjerulf's book Happy Hour is 9 to 5 has original suggestions on how to create a happier working ambience and is a great read for team leaders

ABOUT THE AUTHOR

Candela Iglesias Chiesa, a researcher and public health specialist by training, has worked as a team leader and project coordinator within academic institutions, hospitals, and not-for-profit organizations.

She relishes the challenges of leading multidisciplinary teams and bringing together highly skilled professionals with different personalities and backgrounds. She is also passionate about using research and evidence to improve strategies and programmes. You can learn more about her work at www.candela-iglesias.com.

Candela carried out her Ph.D. research at the Pasteur Institute in Paris, and earned a Master in Public Health from the London School of Hygiene and Tropical Medicine.

She has lived and worked in Mexico, South Africa, France, and Norway. She's an avid hiker and enjoys obstacle-course racing and scuba diving.

59364642R00151

Made in the USA
San Bernardino, CA
04 December 2017